Sports Legends

A History of Minnesota Sports

By Phil Tippin

150 YEARS
of STATEHOOD
1858 · 2008

Welcome to *Sports Legends*

In *Sports Legends,* the sixth book in The Minnesota Series, you'll find stories and rare photographs of your favorite sports figures in Minnesota. Inside, relive the drama and heroics of some of the greatest athletes to ever grace the playing fields, stadiums and arenas of the state. Previous books in the series include *Storms!, Music Legends, Media Tales, Storms 2* and *Famous Crimes.* Pick up books at retailers across the state or order online at www.minnesotaseries.com.

Author **Phil Tippin**
Design and Layout **Phil Tippin**
Proofreader **Marsha Kitchel**
Web Consultant **Risdall Advertising, New Brighton, Minn.**
Printing **Bolger: Vision Beyond Print, Minneapolis, Minn.**
Photographs **D Media Services**
Publishers **D Media: Debra Gustafson Decker, Dale Decker**

(952) 926-3950. dmedia@juno.com.
Books available at www.minnesotaseries.com

ISBN 9780978795665

Library of Congress Control Number: 2008935917

Contents

Foreword

I'm not a "homer" but I did grow up a Viking fan. I can remember hustling home after church on fall Sundays to watch the Vikings on CBS. This was before the NFL Network, ESPN, even cable television. You got one game and more times than not, it was the Vikings. I'm talking the glory years of the 1970s. My dad was a Bears fan, so when those two teams played it was an extra special Sunday.

Fran Tarkenton was my favorite football player growing up and I would spend hours imitating those amazing scrambles in my front yard. I miss that pure joy of sports. Even though I'm closer to the action, closer than I ever dreamed I would be, it's more of a job than being a true fan.

But, that's what's amazing about a book like this. It triggers memories and feelings we experienced growing up as fans. Whether it was Fran Tarkenton, Bill Goldsworthy or the '91 Twins, we remember. I know there's a generation of Minnesota sports fans that has never heard of the Minneapolis Millers in baseball or the Fighting Saints in hockey. That's sad, but there's still time to catch up with the rest of us. Read and enjoy.

Randy Shaver, Anchor, KARE-11 Sports, Minneapolis-St. Paul

Ernie Nevers, Minnesota's first football star. (Courtesy of the Chicago Historical Society)

Chapter 1

The Barnstormers
The Duluth Eskimos and the Birth of the National Football League

Duluth was a good place to own a hardware store in the 1920s. The nation was enjoying a vigorous economy, and the port city was busy as Iron Range taconite was much in demand in those industrial-revolution days. The Duluth Kelley Hardware store sponsored team sports clubs in the area as a means to promote their business. With a surplus of dock workers, there was no shortage of talent for their teams.

College football in the day was big business. Ivy League schools held sway while state universities in the Big Ten and around the country were building formidable programs. The performances of the Four Horsemen, Jim Thorpe and Red Grange dazzled large crowds and captured headlines. Playing for a top school was considered the pinnacle of an athlete's success. After graduation these athletes were considered privileged to use their degree to get a well-paying job and career in the business world. Professional baseball and boxing offered good wages for some, while pro football had yet to become a viable option.

In reality, maybe not all of the athletes who played college ball were meant for the business world, some may have just needed extra money. Whatever the case, it became common for college players to moonlight by playing football for a paycheck. Though this practice was hardly a secret, it was against NCAA rules and players performed under assumed names. Though the addition of an occasional ringer or two was the norm, whole teams would sometimes tap the free market. It was reported that teams from Notre Dame and Illinois matched up as did Michigan and Ohio State for contests under assumed *team* names.

The '20s was a time of opportunity everywhere and entrepreneurs began to see promise in professional football. Small franchises were started around the country and loosely-organized leagues were formed. This was a time when teams that play today got their start. The Chicago Bears, Green Bay Packers and New York Giants were part of the early leagues as George Halas, "Curly" Lambeau and others played and worked the business of keeping their teams afloat. This was a time of teams from Racine, Rock Island, Evanston, Dayton, Canton and elsewhere. As teams began popping up, owners worked to establish organization, forming the National Football League in the summer of 1922.

The Minnesota Vikings weren't the first NFL team from the state. That distinction belongs to the Twin Cities' Minneapolis Marines. The next year another Minnesota team joined the NFL—the Duluth Kelleys.

As with their other sponsored teams, the four partners of Kelley Hardware ponied up the league entry fee and bought uniforms. To compete, they signed some former college stars, including Duluth's Dewey Scanlon of Valparaiso and Joey Sternaman from the University of Illinois. Over a hundred former college players and dock workers attended tryouts. They played their home games at Athletic Park, a minor league baseball stadium located near the ore docks of the port city.

In their first season, the Kelleys won their first four games (two against the Minneapolis Marines), lost their next three (one to the Green Bay Packers), and finished the year 4-3, good enough for seventh place. The Kelleys were a tough bunch and their defense was outstanding. Their games were close and low-scoring.

In the next year the upstarts from Duluth performed better, finishing 5-1 (again losing to the Packers) and fourth in the league. But the business of football started to suffer in 1925, and with the team running out of money, the Kelleys played only three games, losing all three. The team would have folded if not for Ole Haugsrud.

Ole Haugsrud began volunteering for the Kelleys before the 1924 season as the team secretary-treasurer. In previous years he had organized a traveling basketball team in the area and knew some of the intricacies of running and promoting professional sports. To keep the team going, Haugsrud was successful in converting the Kelleys to a player-owned team where players would pay to play and divide the gate after each game.

As finances began to tighten across the league in 1925, there was one shining example of success and Haugsrud took notice. The Chicago Bears' owner George Halas signed three-time All American Red Grange of the University of Illinois. The "Galloping Ghost" was the most famous—and talented—football player of his day. With Grange, the Bears enjoyed success on the field and enormous attendance. The contrast between the Chicago team and the 0-3 Kelleys was apparent.

After the season, with players disenchanted with ownership of the club, Haugsrud took over the floundering Duluth franchise, along with Dewey Scanlon. Ole knew his team had two problems. Located in Duluth, cost-conscious teams from the league were loathe to make the long trip north to face the Kelleys. Also, they didn't have a bona fide star attraction to draw the gate needed. Ole had a solution.

The terrain of professional football changed after the 1925 season. After the Bears' success, Grange bargained for a new contract. Failing that, he and his manager formed a new league, the American Football League. The AFL was well-funded and offered big contracts to college football stars across the country. The new Brooklyn franchise signed Notre Dame's Four Horsemen, naming the team the Brooklyn Horsemen. With the exception of Grange himself, no star was bigger than Stanford's All American and former Superior, Wisconsin star Ernie Nevers.

With the new league offering serious competition, the NFL started the next season with twenty-two strong franchises. Forecasts dimmed, however, when the AFL's Chicago Cardinals announced they had signed Nevers. Ole Haugsrud, sensing that the deal hadn't been finalized, met with Nevers to try to change his mind. As it turned out, Haugsrud had lived near Nevers growing up and was able to sign him by matching the Cardinals' offer. NFL president Joe Carr, hearing of Ole's feat, proclaimed that Haugsrud had saved the NFL.

With his star signed, the Duluth owner arranged to play most of his team's games on the road so they could play better teams in larger venues and take advantage of their new notoriety. With an eye on promotion, he also changed the name of the team to Ernie Nevers' Duluth Eskimos. New uniforms were the first in the league to sport a team logo. Custom mackinaw coats in team colors were procured to keep the players warm on the sidelines. Before the '26 season, Haugsrud arranged for the team to participate in a training camp (at Two Harbors, Minn.), a first-of-its-kind innovation for the league.

The Eskimos returned several players from previous years including Russ Method, "Doc" Williams and Dewey Scanlon. Added to the team was the colorful and talented Johnny "Blood" McNally at halfback. With Nevers playing fullback and the gritty, lightning-fast McNally in the backfield, the Eskimos were a potent force.

Duluth opened at home with a win over the Kansas City Cowboys, an NFL traveling team with speed, talent and a flair for promotion. After the game, the Eskimos became a traveling team themselves, playing thirteen more league games and fifteen exhibitions before they returned home four months later. In the standings, they won more than they lost. In touring from Chicago to New York, Detroit to Kansas City, the Bears were the only team to beat them decisively. More than that, the Eskimos were entertaining, and finally profitable.

The next season the Eskimos won just one game but the team continued to profit. In the spring, Nevers switched sports to pitch for the St. Louis Browns. After the baseball season was over, he returned to football, coaching at Stanford.

With Nevers gone, Haugsrud expected financial losses and suspended the Eskimos' operations. Players dispersed to other teams and the franchise was bought later and became the Orange (NJ) Tornadoes, later developing into today's Washington Redskins. As part of the sale, Ole insisted on an option to bid on the next NFL franchise granted in the state of Minnesota. In 1961, a prescient Haugsrud became ten-percent owner of the Minnesota Vikings.

Later, Ernie Nevers and Blood McNally joined fellow Minnesotan, Bronko Nagurski, in the first class of the Pro Football Hall of Fame in 1963, immortalizing Nevers, the Eskimos and the early years of the NFL. Ernie Nevers passed away in 1973. His legacy and the Eskimos' history lives in books and movies, including George Clooney's 2007 cinematic release "Leatherheads." The Nevers name surfaced again in Minnesota sports as descendants Gordy, and later, Tom Nevers, each played professional baseball.

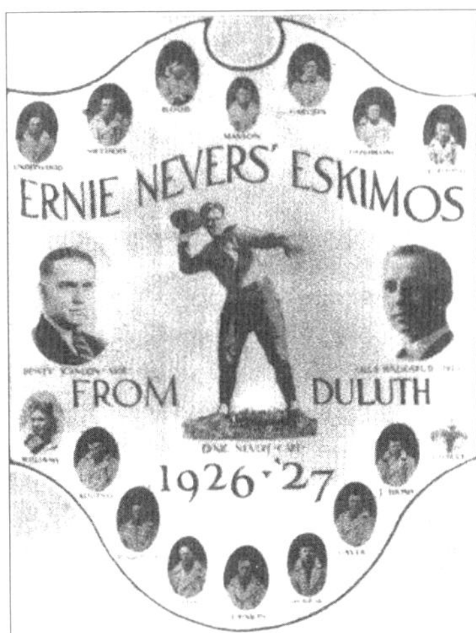

Clockwise from top left: John "Blood" McNally starred for the Eskimos; poster featuring Ernie Nevers, Manager Dewey Scanlon and President Ole Haugsrud. Haugsrud later owned part of the Vikings and a stadium in Superior, Wisconsin bears his name; the barnstorming Eskimos' travel trunk.

Clockwise from top left: Red Grange and George Halas provided opposition for the Eskimos; Halas' Chicago Bears transcended eras from the Eskimos to today's Vikings; The Duluth waterfront of the early 1900s, home to the Eskimos' Athletic Park.

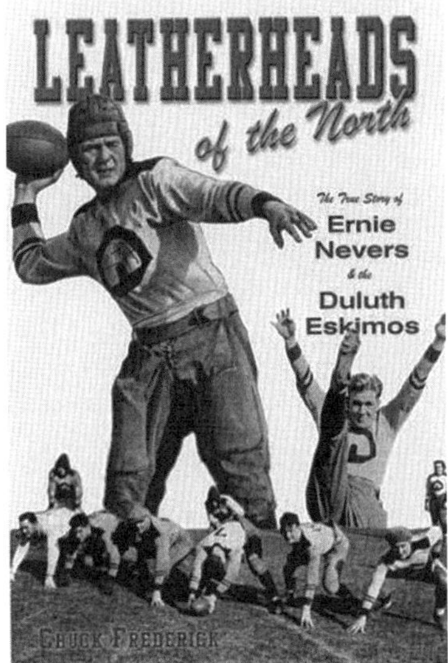

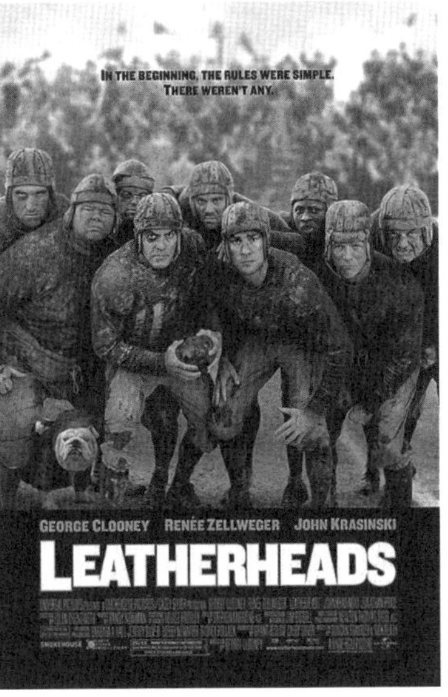

Clockwise from top left: An Eskimos' sideline coat kept the players warm; Ernie Nevers publicity shot; books and movies about the Eskimos include *Leatherheads of the North* and George Clooney's *Leatherheads*.

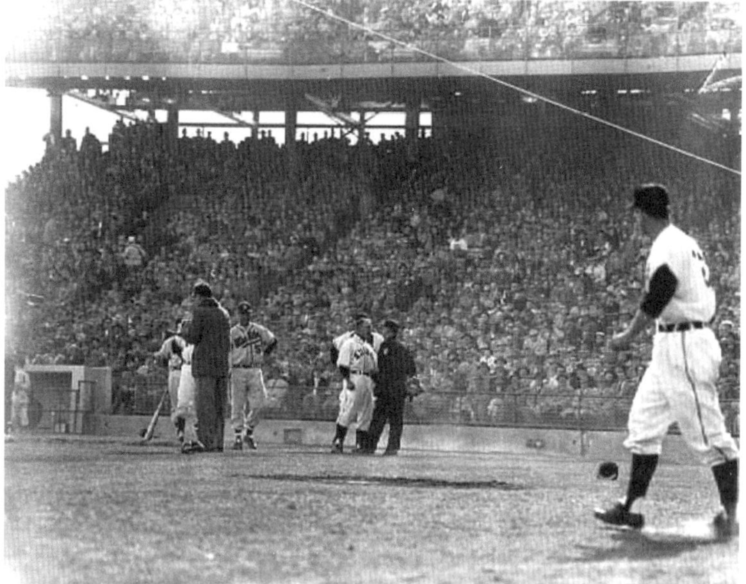

The Saints and Millers entertained Minnesota's baseball fans through the 1950s.

Crosstown Rivals
The Minneapolis Millers and St. Paul Saints

The Minneapolis Millers and St. Paul Saints baseball teams played in the American Association for fifty-nine years. During that time the Millers won 4,800 games, the Saints, 4,719. The teams battled on the field or in the won-loss columns for league championships. For the Twin Cities, this great rivalry stoked legends, spawned careers and ultimately led to a Minnesota team in the major leagues.

The Millers and Saints were part of the struggling Western League before the American Association formed in 1902. The new league was formed to protect teams from being raided by the major leagues for players. They gathered with similar leagues on the East and West Coasts under the National Association in 1904. These were considered the first, legitimate minor league organizations and were now considered part of "organized baseball."

The Saints of the 1890s were owned by Charles Comisky. In 1899 he moved them to Chicago where they became the White Sox. The Saints entered the league as the St. Paul Apostles before reverting back to Saints years later.

The Millers played at Nicollet Park, located on the corner of Nicollet Ave. and 31st St. in Minneapolis, across from today's K Mart. While still close enough to downtown, the site was chosen for its proximity to the Lake Street rail line. The Saints played at Lexington Park, in the St. Paul Midway at the corner of Universty

Ave. and Lexington, on the University streetcar line. Both parks grew to seat 10,000 fans. Lexington had a mammoth outfield while Nicollet was compact by comparison.

Fans of all stripes filled the stands of both teams, from gamblers to businessmen, from families to barflies. Though both had covered bleachers, both fields would quickly turn to mud when it rained. Fans were quick to respond to bad calls or unsportsmanlike behavior from opposing teams; they would show their displeasure by throwing eggs, stones and bricks at umpires and players. Fights were common and police were called in for on-field brouhahas. Players spiked and threw sand in the faces of their opponents. Grudges were formed. The Minneapolis and St. Paul rivalry was already like dynamite and the Saints and Millers served as the wick.

From the outset, the Saints were strong, winning the eight-team league title in 1903 and '04. Borne of playing in Lexington Park, the team hit for percentage—not power—and were great baserunners, the small-ball team of the early 1900s. The Saints had a future Hall of Famer in second baseman Miller Huggins, who would later go on to manage the powerhouse Yankees of the '20s.

After the 1904 season, the Saints headed east on a barnstorming tour, playing American Association runner-up Columbus in Ohio and the Eastern league champs, the Buffalo Bisons. This run out east became the cornerstone for a championship series between the leagues that was known as the Little World Series and later the Junior World Series.

The Millers took awhile longer to put together quality teams. After some reorganization in 1904, they began a slow climb to the first division, winning their first title in 1910 and repeating the next two years. The team was considered the best of that period and featured some future Hall inductees of their own. In 1909, the Millers were home to a young left-handed pitcher named Cy Young, who would go on to set the record for most career wins in the majors with 511. Young won both games of a double header against the Milwaukee Brewers that year, both shutouts. Another Miller pitcher, Urban "Red" Faber, went on to start with the White Sox. Minneapolis caught another Hall of Famer on his way down in Rube Waddell, formerly of the Philadelphia Athletics who came to the Millers in 1911 and pitched over two seasons. The free-spirited Waddell, who left the Athletics after finding himself at odds with manager Connie Mack, pitched a shutout for the team in 1913, one year before his death in 1914, from tuberculosis.

The Saints and Millers didn't really lock horns until the 1915 season when both were first-place contenders. After sluggish starts, both teams began to rise in the standings by mid-year, with the Saints closing in on first place. In July, the teams played a close series, with the Saints winning three of five. By that time, fans rode Twin Cities' streetcars across the river for away games. Streetcars added tradition to the dynasty. Fans made a day of it, fueled by anticipation and competition. During a long road trip late in the season, more seating was added to Lexington Park to accommodate the Saints' growing fan base. By the end of the year, the Millers and Saints were regularly dispatching other teams in the league but couldn't shake each other, with the Saints holding the lead. At the end, the Millers overtook the Saints for the title. But the Saints were on the verge of putting together a great lineup over the next couple of years, teams that were considered among the best in the history of the minor leagues.

The St. Paul team of 1920 was stacked. Their solid infield included Leo Dressen and power hitter Goldie Rapp. Bruno Haas, a former Philadelphia Athletic joined the outfield while Charley Hall led a group of three 20-game-winning pitchers. The Saints finished with an incredible 115-49 record, 28 games ahead of second place Louisville, but lost the Little World Series to the Baltimore Orioles, the powerful Independent (formerly Eastern) league champ. Averaging over six runs per game, the '20 Saints routinely drubbed the competition. They won the American Association crown again in 1921, '22 and '24, finally winning the Little World Series against the Orioles that year.

The farm system began to develop in the minors in the mid-'20s. Though minor league teams were independent, player development arrangements between minor and major league teams developed. The Saints struck an informal working relationship with New York, which allowed St. Paul to be compensated for feeding players to the Yankees, while enjoying the occasional benefits of having a big-leaguer on the club for development. Yankees sent to St. Paul in that period included pitcher "Lefty" Gomez and shortstop Leo Durocher, both later Hall of Famers.

As the ties with the majors became stronger, the Twin Cities enjoyed barnstorming tours by major league stars. Babe Ruth brought the Yankees to Lexington Park in 1926 and '27 with the Saints losing to the famed "Murderers' Row" lineup (which included Lou Gehrig) 9-8 in the latter matchup. St. Paul also hosted an exhibition game with the St. Louis Cardinals World Championship "Gashouse Gang." Ruth returned a year after his retirement to play an exhibition game at Nicollet Park in which he played half the game for the Millers and the other half for the Saints. Ruth lobbied to become manager of the Saints at the time but inexplicably, the Saints declined.

In 1932, Minneapolis put together a strong team of its own, featuring a big-time home run hitter in Joe Hauser. Traded from Baltimore, Hauser led the Independent League in homers the previous two years, including an incredible 63 in 1930. The team also enjoyed the addition of infielders "Babe" Ganzel and Andy Cohen to a lineup that, along with Hauser, Ernie Smith and Joe Mowry, set the record for runs in a season for the duration of the American Association. Scoring over seven runs a game, they won the title easily before falling to the Newark Bears in the Junior (formerly Little) World Series. Hauser hit 49 homers that year but that was nothing in comparison to 1934. In 1934, despite getting off to a slow start and suffering a knee injury at the end of the year, Hauser set the all-time home run record of 69. He also led the Association in runs scored, runs batted in, walks and total bases. The powerful Minneapolis team won again that season and again in '35, but fell to the Columbus Red Birds in the Series both years.

With the success of both franchises, the rivalry continued to grow between the Saints and Millers. Lights were added to both of their stadiums in the late '30s and games between the teams grew in intensity. Fans looked forward to "home and away" double headers on Memorial Day, the Fourth of July and Labor Day in which the teams would play at one park in an afternoon game at one stadium and then a later game at the other.

As ownership and management changed in baseball and the farm system continued to develop, more big names played with the Millers and Saints. In 1938, a young Ted Williams saw duty for Minneapolis, though the Saints had the better team. The future all-time great led the league in batting average, home runs and RBIs before joining the Boston Red Sox the next year. In one jaw-dropping performance, Williams hit a Nicollet Park homer so far that it cleared Nicollet Avenue to land on the roof of a building across the street. To help train Williams and the rest of the team, the Millers made good use of legend Rogers Hornsby as their hitting coach. Minneapolis also had baseball lifers like Wayne Tewilliger and Gene Mauch and some star power in pitcher Eddie Stanky. Future Dodger great Duke Snider was a member of the powerful Saints teams of the '40s. The Saints also had manager Walter Alston, shortstop Don Zimmer and outfielder Bill Sharman, who went on to star with basketball's Boston Celtics. But if the farm system fed the big leagues, it also served to break the color line.

Brooklyn Dodgers owner Branch Rickey was instrumental in bringing Jackie Robinson to the big leagues. Rickey was also keen on the development of another black player, Roy Campanella, whom he sent to the Saints in 1948 to integrate minor league baseball. Campanella, the first black player in the American Association, was called up later in the year and went on to win three league MVP awards with the Dodgers. That Saints team also had Dan Bankhead, who later became the first black pitcher in the majors. The Millers won the pennant in 1950 behind the play of former Negro League star Ray Dandrige at third base. They looked to repeat as champs with the signing of center fielder Willie Mays. The "Say Hey" Kid piled up big numbers at the plate with a .477 batting average, and made stellar plays in center field. By midseason he was called up by the recently relocated Giants of San Francisco. Outfielder Monte Irvin led the Millers to the pennant in '55 while Orlando Cepeda starred in 1957.

The expansion-minded 1950s had the Twin Cities yearning for the major leagues. Groups from St. Paul and Minneapolis broke ground to build stadiums to lure a franchise. In St. Paul they built the original Midway Stadium, a modern ballpark that was second to none. The Minneapolis group built Metropolitan Stadium in Bloomington. The teams took to their new fields in 1956.

The Millers shut down Nicollet Park the year before with their first Junior World Series championship and brought a solid team to the Met. That period saw the great Carl Yastrzemski in a Millers uniform and coach Jimmie Foxx with the club. The success of the team continued with notoriety as Minneapolis faced Fidel Castro's Havana Sugar Kings in the Junior World Series in 1959 with games at Cuba's Gran Stadium, and Metropolitan Stadium.

In an effort to squelch the emergence of a third major league, the Continental League, the majors expanded. The American League installed a new team in Washington, D.C.

and sent the existing Senators to the Twin Cities. Met Stadium and its backers won the franchise, and in a concession to St. Paul, named the team the Minnesota Twins. The Saints and Millers folded operations after the 1960 season. The Twins began play in 1961.

The original Midway Stadium, near Energy Park in St. Paul, was torn down for lack of use. The current, smaller Midway Stadium, built across Snelling Avenue, is the host to a new St. Paul Saints franchise that was assembled in the early '90s by Mike Veeck, son of former White Sox owner Bill Veeck, with partner Bill Murray of *Saturday Night Live* fame. The current Saints team has had its share of stars in uniform too, including the Cubs' Leon "Bull" Durham and Jack Morris. Outfielder Daryl Strawberry recovered his game in time with the Saints for a World Series ring with the Yankees. An independent Millers team briefly played at Parade Stadium in 1994. They changed their name to the Loons and departed in 1995. Meanwhile, with the planned groundbreaking of a new stadium in Burnsville to host a new Millers team in 2009, another Saints-Millers rivalry cannot be far behind.

Top: This Millers team includes a young Carl Yastzremski.
Bottom: The 1952 St. Paul Saints.

Clockwise from top left: Joe Hauser was the "Home Run King" for the Millers; Willie Mays, Carl Yaztremski and Wayne Terwilliger all played in the Twin Cities. Terwilliger went on to coach for the Twins and the modern-day Saints.

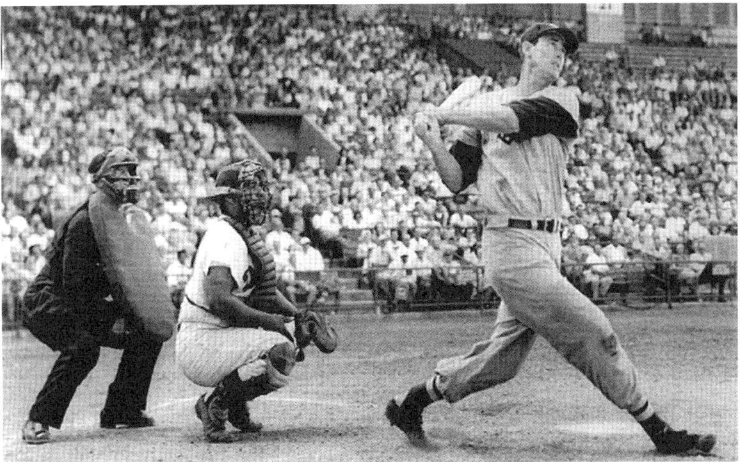

Top: Ted Williams and Roy Campanella (here on the cover of *Life* magazine) played for the Millers and Saints respectively on the way to the Hall of Fame.
Bottom: The two met as big-leaguers with Campanella behind the plate as Williams took a swing during a spring training game.

Cloudy

Minneapolis Morning Tribune

Washington Senators Move to Twin Cities in '61

Budget Data Due Next Week

2 Airmen Killed in Crash of Jet Near Wold Field

City Sets Maximum Tax Rate

Other Baseball Stories in Sports Peach

American League to Expand

Summit Cost U.S., Russia Prestige Loss

Top: The Saints are pictured near the end, playing at old Midway Stadium in St.Paul.
Below: Newspaper headlines spelled the end of an era.

Top: The modern Saints team has boasted the likes of Daryl Strawberry and the antics of owner Mike Veeck. Bottom: Rendering of the proposed stadium for a revived Millers team to play in Burnsville.

Bronco Nagurski was one of the greatest athletes of his time.

Chapter 3

Giants of the North
Minnesota Golden Gopher Football from the '30s to the '60s

In the Golden Age of Radio, college—not professional—football dominated the sport. At the time, the college game was rivaled in popularity only by major league baseball, horse racing and boxing. This was an era when legends were born: Red Grange at Illinois, Knute Rockne rode the Four Horsemen to championships at Notre Dame, the gargantuan "Big House" showcased perennial winners at the University of Michigan. This was an era when the Minnesota Golden Gophers won five national championships under coach Bernie Bierman and produced a player who many consider to be the greatest to ever play the game, Bronko Nagurski.

The Gophers were one of the top teams of the day, much like Ohio State and USC are now. The Gopher teams from 1900-1921, coached by Dr. Henry L. Williams, enjoyed success and notoriety, with eight first-place finishes in the Big Ten including five undefeated seasons in that period. Enthusiasm for the team was high. After World War I, University of Minnesota officials committed to building a new stadium to showcase their team, as many other schools did around the country.

Memorial Stadium, the "Brick House," was completed in October of 1924 and seated over fifty-five thousand. At a time when the University of Michigan was building the 72,000-seat Michigan Stadium, and the University of Southern

California was playing at Memorial Coliseum, Memorial Stadium joined a list that served to inspire millions of college football fans.

The first star to shine on the Memorial Stadium stage was a farmhand from up north: Bronislau "Bronko" Nagurski, who began playing for the "U" in 1927. As the story goes, Minnesota Head Coach Clarence Spears had gotten lost on a recruiting trip near International Falls when he stopped to ask directions from a farmhand working in a field. In response, the farmhand lifted his plow to point to the direction of town. The farmhand, Nagurski, was signed on the spot to a full football scholarship at the "U."

Nagurski was a mythological presence on a pretty good team. While the Gophers were a respectable 18-4-2 during his run with the Maroon and Gold, Bronko Nagurski was incredible. In a 1928 game against top-ranked Wisconsin, Nagurski led the team to a win with a forced and recovered fumble, a game-saving tackle and a last-second interception—all while wearing a metal brace to protect broken ribs. In 1929 he was named an All-American on both offense (as a fullback) and on defense at tackle.

But while the great Nagurski was not part of Minnesota's greatest teams, he did set the table. Enter Bernie Bierman, who coached the Gophers to five national titles and six Big Ten titles in his first ten years at Minnesota. This was the Golden Era of University of Minnesota football.

Bernie Bierman took the reigns at Minnesota in 1932 after head coaching jobs at the University of Montana, Mississippi State and Tulane—where he guided the Green

Wave to the Rose Bowl against USC in 1931. Bierman inherited a team that finished in the middle of the pack the year before, as would his '32 team. But in his first two years Bierman laid the groundwork for the Gophers to become the most dominant team of the 1930s.

Bernie grew up in Litchfield and played for the Gophers in 1915, where he earned All-Conference honors at tailback. He served in the Marines in World War I before returning home to a career in football.

Bierman's approach to discipline was legendary. Nicknamed the "Grey Eagle" because of his no-nonsense demeanor and prematurely gray hair, his teams worked hard to be better prepared physically and mentally to play the game. His approach to training was grueling, and penalties for mental errors severe. Bierman believed in simple, common-sense football.

Minnesota was home to some of the best football prospects of the day and the new home-grown coach was very effective in recruiting that local talent. During his career at Minnesota, Bierman coached twenty-one All Americans including stars such as Ed Widseth, Bud Wilkinson, Ray King and Bill Bevan. Returning for Bierman's first season were stars Francis "Pug" Lund at halfback and Frank Larson at end.

An unlikely promoter, he was credited with changing the school colors to include gold in his first year, giving Minnesota the maroon and gold scheme that has become so much a part of the school's identity.

After a 5-3 record in his first season, and enjoying an oddly undefeated '33 season at 4-0-4, Bierman's system and recruiting class made the Gophers a strong two-deep at every position for the upcoming year. So overpowering was Bierman's squad that in 1934 they outscored their opponents 270-38. That year, sportswriter Grantland Rice considered naming the whole starting lineup to the All American team. Minnesota went 8-0, including a 34-0 thrashing of Michigan in front of 60,000 fans at Memorial Stadium to win the national championship.

The outlook for the '35 season was not as good and Bierman worked to rebuild the team after losing eleven players, including Lund, Bill Bevan and Bob Tenner. The Gophers' revamped team featured players who would become stars in their own right: Ray King at end, tackles Ed Widseth and Dick Smith, and Wilkinson at guard. The games were closer than the year before, witnessed by a 12-7 win early in the season at Nebraska. But the Gophers were unbeaten through the first six games before blowing out Michigan at Ann Arbor and Wisconsin at home to complete another undefeated season and Big Ten title.

The stakes were raised for the Gophers in 1936 as the team carried three years of undefeated football into the season and added the Universities of Washington and Texas to the schedule. Bierman moved Wilkinson to quarterback to shore up a backfield that included fullback Andy Uram. After two close games against Washington and Nebraska, the team easily dispatched Michigan and Purdue at the "Brick House" to go 4-0.

The next week, on a rainy Halloween in Evanston, their winning streak ended and their title hopes were placed in jeopardy as they fell to Northwestern in a close and controversial game. Minnesota was so vexed by the upset that they humiliated a good Iowa team 52-0 the next week. Convincing wins over Texas and Wisconsin finished the year and their one-loss record was enough to crown them champs again.

Bierman's teams lost two games in each of the '37 and '38 seasons but retained their formidable stature in college football, winning the Big Ten both years. The run seemed over in 1939 as the team stumbled to a losing record despite a roster that included running backs Sonny Franck and Bruce Smith.

But the run was not over. Behind the play of All Americans Smith, Franck, Urban Odson, and Dick Wildung, the Gophers went undefeated again in 1940 and '41, winning eight games both seasons. Except for the Purdue game, all of the games in 1940 were close, especially a 7-6 home win against a third-ranked Michigan team. The following year the Gophers were tested by Michigan, Northwestern and Nebraska in the middle of the schedule, on their way to the last of Bernie Bierman's championship years.

Bierman left the "U" to join the Marines at the beginning of World War II. He returned after the war and had some success before ending his career in 1950. But the Golden Era—Bierman's era—was over. In all, he coached the Gophers to five national championships with five undefeated teams. The University of Minnesota football program remains the last to win three national titles in a row.

In the years following Bierman's departure, Minnesota football declined. New coach Wes Fesler finished no higher than fifth in the Big Ten during his run. Fesler was fired after his third season, leading to speculation that the team would hire the popular former Gopher great Bud Wilkinson to right the ship. Instead, the "U" hired unknown Mississippi State coach Murray Warmath to lead the team in 1954.

In his eleven seasons at Minnesota, Warmath had some good years, including the last Minnesota national title in 1960 and a Rose Bowl appearance in 1961. Warmath also had some bad years, such as the one-win season of 1958. Despite the disarray he found in taking over the program, he discovered he was left with a few good players from Fesler's teams. With the familiar staff of coaches that he had brought from Mississippi, Warmath was able to install his system quickly and go on to a surprising 7-2 year. Fullback Bob McNamara received honors in leading the team to a Top-20 finish.

If a 7-2 season was just enough to earn the tolerance of Gopher fans who had hoped for the hiring of Wilkinson, the years to come would test that tolerance. The next season was an abysmal three-win year, followed by a job-saving campaign in '56. In the next three years Minnesota would win seven games. To save his job, Warmath turned to out-of-state recruits and did what only a handful of major college football programs were doing at the time to compete: He began to recruit black athletes.

While the color barrier began to fall in earnest in the late 1950s, there weren't very many black athletes on football teams at the nation's largest schools. Warmath was from the South, having played college ball for General Robert Neyland and the Tennessee Volunteers.

The southern schools were especially slow to add African Americans to their teams so Warmath used his connections there to land future NFL Hall of Fame defensive ends Bobby Bell and Carl Eller, both from North Carolina. From Pennsylvania, the Gophers landed quarterback Sandy Stephens along with halfbacks Judge Dickson and Bill Munsey. Along with the other out-of-state recruits and returning players, like All American guard Tom Brown, Warmath hoped to turn things around.

The 1960 Gophers proved to be great on both sides of the ball. Led by Brown, the defense was stubborn on the field and stingy on the scoreboard. The offense, with Stephens at the helm, could score points by the bucket. By the time the national media took notice, Warmath's squad was 6-0, and ranked #3 in the country as they faced #1 Iowa in Minneapolis. Tom Brown made the difference that day, dominating the line of scrimmage as the Gophers beat the Hawkeyes and claimed top spot in the polls. The team had a letdown the following week with a loss to an overachieving Purdue team, but rebounded the final week of the season with a convincing win over Wisconsin to finish the year with an 8-1 record and regain the #1 ranking in the polls. The Gophers were voted national champs before their loss to Washington in the Rose Bowl. Coach Murray Warmath, who so desperately needed redemption, got all he needed.

The 1961 team lost their first and last games of the year, against Missouri and Wisconsin at the “Brick House,” and won everything in between to earn their second consecutive Rose Bowl appearance. This time they won the game over

UCLA. Tom Brown was lost to graduation but the recruiting class from the previous year of Bell, Eller and Stephens were special standouts. Bell and Stephens were All Americans that year and Stephens was the Rose Bowl MVP. Warmath was named Coach of the Year. It was the last year that the Gophers went to the Rose Bowl

1962 was another winning year for the Gophers and the '67 club went 8-2 to share the Big Ten title. But the days of titles and championships were soon gone for Murray Warmath and the University of Minnesota football program. Warmath retired in 1971, and with him, the last great teams in Gopher football history.

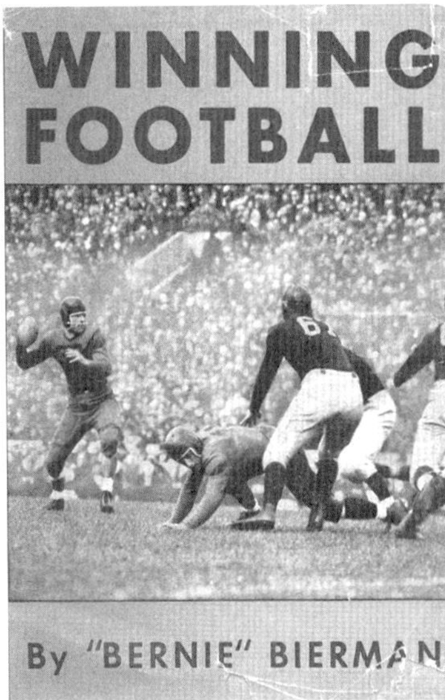

Bernie Bierman wrote foootball books and coached the Gophers to prominence at Memorial Stadium.

Top: Nagurski shows his All-American form at fullback. (Courtesy of the Chicago Historical Society) Bottom: Pug Lund and Bud Wilkinson starred for the Gophers.

Top: Bierman with his team before practice.
Bottom: Lund and Bierman accept the Little Brown Jug after a win over Michigan; the Floyd of Rosedale trophy was awarded to the victor of games with rival Iowa.

Clockwise from top left: Gophers stars George Franck, Bruce Smith, Biggie Munn and Paul Giel. Smith won the Heisman in 1941.

Clockwise from top left: Longtime Gophers' broadcaster Ray Christiansen and gridiron star Bob McNamara inspired fans on radio and at the games.

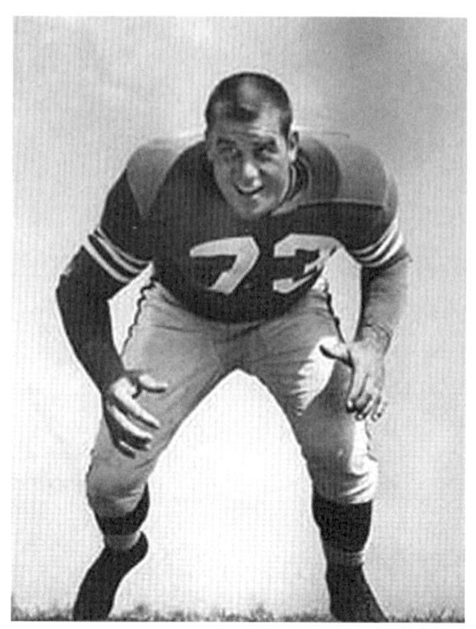

Clockwise from top left: '50s and '60s-era stars Leo Nomellini, Sandy Stephens, Bobby Bell and Carl Eller. Stephens was a pioneering QB. Bell and Eller starred in the AFL and NFL.

Murray Warmath coached the Gophers into the 1970s.

99

The Minneapolis Lakers
Mr. Basketball and the NBA's First Dynasty

Professional sports as we know them today gained national attention after World War II. It was then that Americans, flush with promise and prosperity, began to look for more entertainment, and new opportunities in business. Though major league baseball was well established, college athletics ruled the day before the war. The post-war years saw the birth of the George Halas-led NFL and a handful of fledgling leagues for professional basketball that merged to form the National Basketball Association.

From the outset of the NBA's first season in 1949-50, one team quickly emerged as a dynasty, not just in that era but for all time: the Minneapolis Lakers. Led by George Mikan, the center dubbed "Mr. Basketball" for his undisputed dominance of the game, the Lakers owned the league with five titles in its first six seasons.

The Lakers came to Minnesota in 1947 when two local businessmen, Ben Berger and Morris Chalfen bought a struggling franchise of the National Basketball League, the Detroit Gems, at the encouragement of Sid Hartman, then a sports writer at the *Minneapolis Tribune*. Owing to financial hardship, the Gems, coming off a 4-40 year, were disbanded by the NBL. Aside from a little equipment, the new owners bought the team in name only.

Berger and Chalfen began building the team by hiring Max Winter, who later went on to own the Minnesota Vikings, as general manager; John Kundla, then coach of St. Thomas College, as coach; and Hartman to run the personnel side of the operation.

Hartman orchestrated a deal to sign former Minnesota Gophers Tony Jaros and Don "Swede" Carlson, veterans from the Chicago Stags of the rival Basketball Association of America, as well as former Gophers Don Smith, Warren Ajax, and Ken Exel. Indiana University star Herm Schaefer was added one game into the season. The first star signed by the team was former Stanford University All American Jim Pollard. Pollard led the Oakland Bittners to the 1946 Amateur Athletic Union championship, and the Lakers agreed to take on three of Pollard's AAU teammates as well. Pollard was considered one of the best forwards of his era and was known for jumping ability that earned him the nickname "The Kangaroo Kid."

In Stew Thornley's *Basketball's Original Dynasty: The History of the Lakers,* Kundla talked about his star. "I can still remember his first game in Oshkosh, I believe," said [Coach] Kundla. "Jim went up for a rebound and pinned it up against the boards. When he returned to the huddle, his elbow was bleeding. I said, 'What happened?' He said, 'I hit my elbow on the backboard.' You didn't see a player do things like that back then."

Though already set with a solid roster, the Lakers became the beneficiaries of the demise of another rival league, the Professional Basketball League of America. Since the Gems had the worst record in that league the previous season, the Gems franchise now owned (as the now renamed Minneapolis Lakers) the first pick in the supplemental draft of unemployed PBLA players. Just four games into their inaugural season, the Lakers gained the rights to league MVP, the center for the Chicago Gears, George Mikan.

Mikan was a 6' 10" giant who had dominated college basketball in his four years at DePaul under coach Ray Meyer. Named College Player of the Year twice and an All American three times, Mikan led DePaul to the NIT title in 1945. On the way to the championship, he broke the collegiate single-game scoring record by putting up 53 points against Rhode Island State, single-handedly outscoring the entire team. He was the first center to use the hook shot, and because of Mikan, goaltending was outlawed, first in college, then the pros.

After losing their first four games after Mikan joined the team, the first-year Lakers ran away with the NBL's Western Division, then dominated the playoffs, winning the best-of-five championship series against the Rochester Royals in four games.

The gold standard of basketball at the time was the Harlem Globetrotters. The Lakers agreed to play the Globetrotters on February 19, 1948 at Chicago stadium as a preliminary game between the Chicago Stags and New York Knicks. Over 17,000 turned out for the double header, a game that the Lakers led at halftime but ended up losing 61-59 on a buzzer-beater to extend the Globetrotters' winning streak to 104 games. Over the ten years that the Lakers played the Globetrotters, the Lakers owned the series, winning six out of the eight games they played.

Following the season the Lakers, Rochester Royals, Fort Wayne Zollner Pistons and Indianapolis Kautskys moved to the Basketball Association of America. The BAA had just finished its second season and had teams in large eastern cities such as New York, Boston and Philadelphia, while NBL teams came from smaller towns such as Moline, Illinois; Anderson, Indiana; and Flint, Michigan. But the NBL did have pro basketball's best teams and players, and the addition of the four NBL teams gave the league the big-name players it needed.

And the biggest name in the league was Mikan, who was the biggest draw in every BAA city. When the Lakers played the New York Knickerbockers that year, the marquee at Madison Square Garden read "George Mikan vs. Knicks."

In the 1949 BAA Playoffs, the Lakers advanced to the finals, where they faced the Washington Capitols, coached by Red Auerbach. Minneapolis opened the best-of-seven series by winning the first three games but in the fourth game Mikan suffered a broken wrist, allowing the Capitols a win. Despite playing the fifth game with a cast on his hand Mikan scored 22 points, but again Washington won. The next game was played in St. Paul, where Minneapolis came away with a 77-56 victory and the BAA Championship.

In the 1949-50 season the NBL merged with the BAA to form the National Basketball Association, the beginning of today's NBA. From the college draft that year, the Lakers added Slater Martin, the All American guard from the University of Texas, and Vern Mikkelsen, center from Hamline University in St. Paul. These players completed the nucleus of a Laker team that would serve as a blueprint for an approach to the game that teams follow to this day.

Also drafted that season was Bud Grant, who went on to coach the Minnesota Vikings. As a reserve, Grant played two seasons with the Lakers before going on to play football for the Philadelphia Eagles of the NFL.

At his natural position in the center, Mikkelsen would see limited playing time, serving as backup to Mikan. In an effort to get him on the floor, Kundla moved Mikkelsen to a forward position, creating basketball's first "power forward." With Mikan now flanked by the 6' 5" Pollard and the 6' 7" Mikkelsen, the modern-day front line of center, power forward and small forward was created.

In *Basketball's Original Dynasty: The History of the Lakers* Mikan said, "You know, there were a lot of things that people don't know about our old Lakers team. People like to think that Red Auerbach and the Celtics never lost, and they were the first dynasty. Well, we beat 'em 16 or 17 straight times, something like that. It's only been recently, what with the NBA's 50th Anniversary celebration, that we've started receiving some recognition for what we did. That makes me feel real good."

In the regular season, playing their home games at the Minneapolis Armory, the Lakers finished with a 51-17 record. In the playoffs they swept the Chicago Stags, Fort Wayne Pistons, and Anderson Packers on the way to the finals. In the first NBA Finals, the Lakers defeated the Syracuse Nationals in six games. In their third year, playing in their third different league, the Lakers won their third straight championship.

In 1950 Mikan was voted the greatest player of the first half of the century by the Associated Press. In *The Vern Mikkelsen Story,* Mikan's frontcourt partner wrote, "In our time, George was Michael Jordan, Magic Johnson and Larry Bird rolled into one," said Mikkelsen. "Everywhere we played, he was who people wanted to see. In fact, he was more acclaimed on both coasts than he was (in Minneapolis). Here, people are more laid-back and they respected his privacy. People talk about all the endorsements players do today, but George was doing that sort of thing even then."

Though the Lakers again reached the finals in 1951, Mikan was injured, and the Lakers' championship streak was interrupted. The season became memorable for the game played on November 22, 1950. It was on that night the Lakers and the Fort Wayne Pistons played the lowest-scoring game in league history, with the Pistons winning 19-18. The slowdown strategy, designed to keep the ball out of Mikan's hands, influenced the league to finally institute a 24-second clock several years later.

The NBA widened the foul lane before the 1951-52 season in an attempt to slow George Mikan, but he still averaged 23 points per game, and finished second in scoring. In the finals, the Lakers and New York Knickerbockers would trade wins and the Lakers emerged with the title in seven games.

Again in 1952-53, the Lakers continued to dominate the league, beating the New York Knickers again for their second straight Championship.

With so much success as head coach, John Kundla received little credit at the time. "Hey," Kundla said, "how can you screw it up when you have Mikan?"

"That's John being too modest," said Mikkelsen. "The hardest thing in the world is to coach that kind of talent and handle the egos. The Xs and Os are the easy part. The hard part is handling the people. My rookie year, I walked into the locker room at halftime and there's John getting on Mikan for something. It didn't matter whether he screwed up or not.

George would always hear it from John, and that's how John sent a message. Nobody was above criticism."

1953-54 proved to be the last championship run for the Lakers as George Mikan developed knee problems. The Lakers signed rookie Clyde Lovellette to spell Mikan, as the Lakers again won their division. In the finals the Syracuse Nationals took the Lakers to seven games before the Lakers came home with their third straight title with an 87-80 win. Following the season, at age 29, Mikan announced his retirement.

In his nine professional seasons, Mikan's teams won seven championships. He led the NBA in scoring three times and in rebounding twice, and he played in the league's first four All Star Games.

Vern Mikkelsen became the name in a trade that would have changed basketball history. Before the 1956-57 season, the Lakers were close to trading Mikkelsen to the Boston Celtics for three players who were in the military. The Lakers likely would have finished with the worst record in the league, giving them the first choice in the draft. The player they wanted was Bill Russell. The Lakers' owners backed out of the deal, giving the St. Louis Hawks, not the Lakers, the rights to Russell. The Hawks then traded him to the Celtics, thus beginning a dynasty.

With the retirement of Mikan and, later, Pollard, the Lakers' fortunes suffered a downturn until the 1958-59 season when they made Elgin Baylor their top draft pick. Baylor dominated the NBA in his first season and won Rookie of the Year. Led by Baylor, the Lakers reached the finals but were swept by the Boston Celtics.

In 1960, the plane taking the Minneapolis Lakers home from St. Louis got lost in the middle of Iowa, without its power generators. The plane's generators had blown shortly after takeoff and the pilot was flying with no radio, no defroster, no heat and no cabin lighting. Concern grew when the scheduled two-hour flight started pushing four hours. With about 30 minutes of gas remaining, the pilot left the decision up to the players—either put the plane down or search for an airport. The decision was made to land the plane, so the pilots lined the plane up to the first open spot they could find and cut the engines. The aircraft finally came to a rest a few feet shy of a steep incline with, miraculously, no injuries aboard. So there, in a cornfield in the middle of Iowa, the Lakers celebrated—with a snowball fight.

Although the team saw some success on the court in its last years in Minneapolis, financial woes caused their owner Bob Short to move the team to Los Angeles in 1960. The team never had a true home, playing games across Minnesota and at Twin Cities' venues. One of their arenas, the Minneapolis Armory, stands today. As Minnesota welcomed new teams in the Twins and Vikings, it said goodbye to the Lakers. Legend has it the new owners of the Vikings bought too much fabric in making the uniforms for their new franchise. Thus, the blue and white of the NBA's first dynasty would become the purple and gold of the new Los Angeles Lakers.

George Mikan went on to become commissioner of the NBA-rival American Basketball Association and passed away in 2005. His statue adorns the lobby of the Target Center in Minneapolis, paying tribute to Minnesota's basketball dynasty of the 1950s.

Clockwise: George Mikan in a publicity shot; Coach John Kundla and the Lakers; the 1953 team lines up.

Clockwise: Vern Mikkelsen, the NBA's first power forward; Slater Martin, and the "almost" Laker, USF's Bill Russell.

Clockwise: Frontmen Jim Pollard and Clyde Lovellette;
the Lakers celebrate another victory.

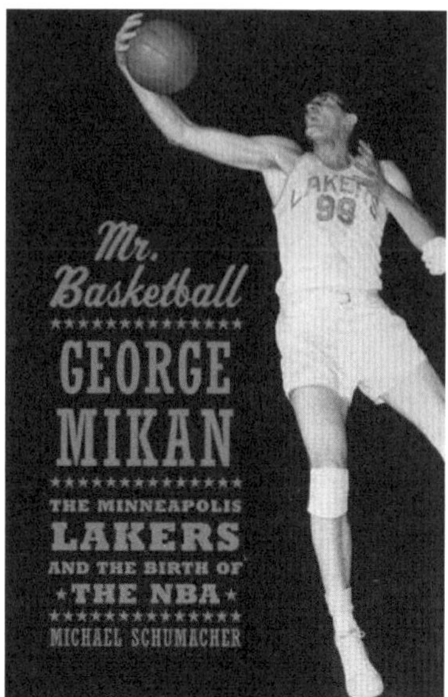

Clockwise: *The Minneapolis Tribune*'s Sid Hartman was the unofficial general manager of the Lakers; George Mikan wrote the book on '50s basketball; the Lakers flew on their own aircraft, a DC3 like the one picture here.

Clockwise from top left: Elgin Baylor went on to star in Los Angeles; Bob Short moved the team to L.A.; the Minneapolis Armory today. When inside, listen closely for the bounce of a ball and the echos of cheers from a bygone era.

Scramblin' Fran
Vikings Legendary Quarterback Fran Tarkenton

You scramble off the busted play, that's all. You do it when you can't do anything else.

– Fran Tarkenton, *Sports Illustrated*

Fran Tarkenton was a gamer. Maybe it came from being the youngest of three boys, always competing with bigger kids in the freewheeling sandlot games of his youth, but the will to compete was always strong in Fran. For Tarkenton, no stranger to preparation and hard work, winning was the goal, and the means was whatever it took.

"Whatever it took" became apparent to his coach, Wally Butts, in Tarkenton's first game at the University of Georgia. The Bulldogs were behind 7-0 to Texas late in the game. After a Longhorn punt, Georgia was pinned down on their own five-yard line. Tarkenton, who had not played in the game, trotted onto the field and took over at quarterback—without the knowledge of the coach. He led his Georgia team on a 95-yard touchdown drive and two-point conversion that won the game for the Bulldogs. "I had been pestering coach Butts to let me go in because that was my personality," said Tarkenton in *Sports Illustrated*. "They wanted to redshirt me and I didn't want to because I thought I could help the team. So I just bolted onto the field. I put myself in."

As a Junior, Tarkenton led Georgia to a 10-1 record and SEC Championship in 1959. In the SEC title game, the

Bulldogs had the ball on the Auburn 13-yard line on fourth down with 30 seconds left in the game. With time-out on the field, Tarkenton diagrammed the game-winning play in the dirt for his offense to win the title.

In his senior year, though his statistics were good, the Bulldogs dropped to 6-4. Pro teams, already concerned about his size—just six feet tall and a little over 180 pounds, lost interest in the Georgia star as the draft approached. In the 1961 draft, he was chosen in the third round by our own Minnesota Vikings of the NFL and in the fifth round of the AFL draft by the Boston (now New England) Patriots. He went to the Vikings.

In Minnesota, the new NFL expansion team was certainly good at promotion, having already sold 27,000 season tickets, but the mix of veterans, cast-offs, untested rookies and walk-ons didn't look too promising as a team. Playing their opening game at home against the powerhouse Chicago Bears guaranteed a good draw at the gate, but didn't make things any easier on the field.

Rookie Tarkenton rode the bench behind former Baltimore Colt George Shaw and figured to have little impact in the game. But impact the game he did. Frustrated with the play of his starter, George Shaw, Coach Norm Van Brocklin brought Tarkenton into the game near the end of the first quarter. When the game was over, Tarkenton had thrown for four touchdowns and run for another as the Vikings won the first game in franchise history 37-13.

The Vikings lost their next seven games but the young quarterback's play attracted attention. Though his passing ability was good and running skills solid, he became known more for his improvisational skills after plays had broken down, often running from sideline to sideline in the backfield, hoping to find an open receiver down the field. Whatever it took. The press gave him the nickname "Scramblin' Fran."

After six uneven years with the Vikings and what became a tumultuous relationship with Van Brocklin, Tarkenton was traded to the New York Giants in 1966. The Giants were a terrible team and excited to have a marquee player to rival the crosstown Jets' "Broadway Joe" Namath. In an article in *Sports Illustrated* before the '67 season, Tarkenton tried to downplay the nickname he had been given:

After the tag "The Scrambler" had become mine, all mine, the public misconceptions about me seemed to multiply. I'd play a game away from home and I'd scramble maybe two or three times, which is my average, and after the game all the reporters would come in and say, "Why didn't you play your usual style?" And, "How come you threw so much from the pocket?" And I would try to say, "I threw from the pocket because that is my style."

"No, it isn't," they would say. "You're a scrambler."

"O.K.," I would say. "I'm a scrambler." Anything to get to the shower.

Though his stay in New York didn't bring many victories to the Giants, Fran's trade sent some valuable draft picks to the Vikings. Players obtained in the trade became key contributors to the Vikings, who were on the rise. Linemen Ron Yary and Ed White, running back Clint Jones and All Pro receiver Bob Grim all played their parts in Vikings fortunes to come. While Tarkenton played for the Giants, the Vikings, led by the famous Purple People Eaters Alan Page, Carl Eller, Jim Marshall and Gary Larsen on defense, won four division titles and went to their first Super Bowl—with the rugged Joe Kapp playing quarterback.

After five frustrating years with the Giants, Tarkenton asked to be traded, handing a list of five contending teams to which he would agree to be traded. One of the teams was the Minnesota Vikings, now coached by Bud Grant. Tarkenton was traded back to Minnesota for quarterback Norm Snead, two first-round draft choices and the very same Bob Grim.

With the addition of Tarkenton and receiver John Gilliam to the '72 team, the Vikings looked good on paper but finished with a sub-par 7-7 record. After years of dependable running from Tommy Mason, Bill Brown and Dave Osborne, the Minnesota running game was in trouble.

That was addressed before the next season as Fran played a huge role in the recruiting of running back Chuck Foreman from the University of Miami. With an elusive running style and ability to catch passes out of the backfield, Foreman earned Rookie of the Year honors while helping to balance a Vikings attack that went 12-2 in the regular season.

Tarkenton guided the Vikings to the Super Bowl that year, their second in five years and his first. While the Vikings dominated the NFC in '73, the Miami Dolphins had completed a perfect season the year before—the only team to ever accomplish that feat—and showed few signs of slowing down. The Dolphins scoring the first 24 points of the game and easily won their second consecutive championship. The

Vikings went to the Super Bowl the following year as well, this time losing to the Pittsburgh Steelers.

After the losses, the feeling in the league was that the 1974-75 season would be the one the Vikings would finally win it all. That feeling was confirmed as Minnesota rolled to an undefeated record in its first ten games. Tarkenton was masterful throughout the year, winning the league's Most Valuable Player award. Their campaign ended before the Super Bowl though, as they fell to the Dallas Cowboys in the conference championship on the controversial "Hail Mary" pass from Cowboys quarterback Roger Staubach to Drew Pearson late in the game in front of a stunned Met Stadium crowd. As the game ended, referee Arman Tersian was felled by debris including a whiskey bottle from the cheap seats. Fran Tarkenton and the Vikings would go to another Super Bowl in 1977, this time losing to the Oakland Raiders, but it was clear that their best years were behind them.

Tarkenton ended his storied football career after the '78 season as one of the most prolific passers in NFL history, throwing 342 touchdown passes and totalling 47,003 yards through the air. Tarkenton also held the NFL rushing record for a quarterback before Randall Cunningham (who would later become a Viking himself) broke that mark. He still holds NFL records for most completed passes and attempted passes in a career.

But if Tarkenton's football career was over, his stay in the limelight was not. A turn as the host for *Saturday Night Live* in 1977 might have paved the way for a new career in television but, regardless, showed that he had a sense of humor. In the opening skit a coach, played by the late John Belushi gives a pep talk to his team before the show:

Coach: *Okay! Good, good, good, good!! Okay, we're good and loose. Okay, let's get together for a team prayer. Get down on one knee. "Dear Lord... please give us the zaniness and courage these men need to make America laugh. Because America is the funniest nation in the world. Help them remember what their coach has told them, so that every man here will have learned something about himself. And please, Lord, help guide Fran Tarkenton... so that he will NOT humiliate himself... like he did... in the Superbowl."*

The 1980s saw Fran on television in stints as a commentator on *Monday Night Football* with Howard Cosell and as co-host of the show, *That's Incredible!* with Kathie Lee Crosby and John Davidson. Tarkenton was Minnesota's first and perhaps greatest sports star to transcend to celebrity status. His business interests also kept him in the spotlight as he promoted his software products KnowledgeWare and, later, the online GoSmallBiz.com. As a motivational speaker he partnered with wellness guru Tony Robbins and currently runs an annuity marketing firm, Tarkenton Financial. In business, as in football, Fran Tarkenton has lived by the words he gave to *Sports Illustrated* at the height of his pro career:

I'll do whatever it takes to get across that goal line. If it's running, if it's passing, if it's scrambling, if it's kicking or crawling or lateraling or standing on my head, I'm willing to do it, and I expect everybody else on the team to feel the same way.

#10 as a Georgia Bulldog and the "Met."

Norm Van Brocklin and his pupil.

Clockwise from top left: Tarkenton's supporting cast in the '60s included Tommy Mason, Bill Brown, Jim Finks and Paul Flatley. Finks was the architect of the '60-70s Vikings.

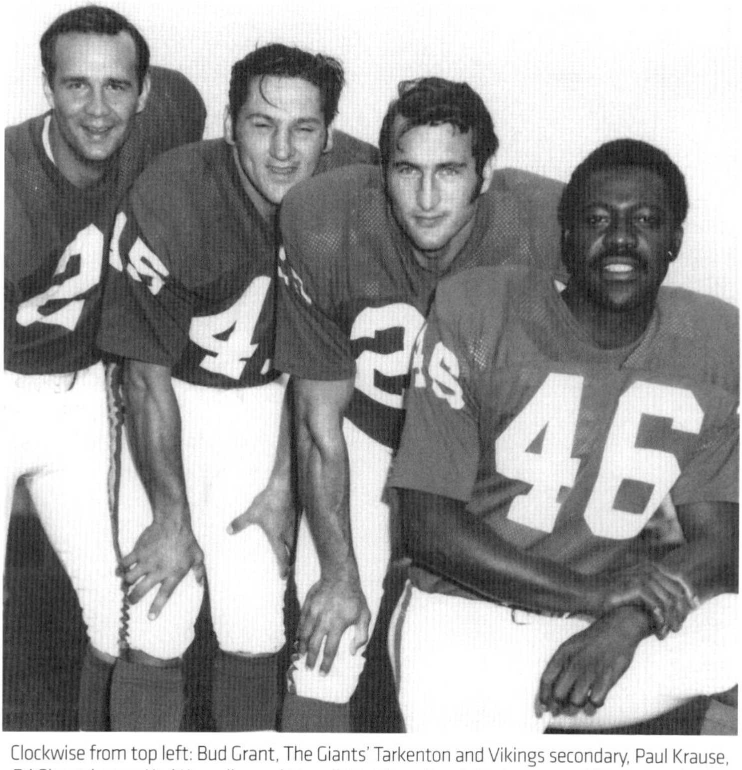

Clockwise from top left: Bud Grant, The Giants' Tarkenton and Vikings secondary, Paul Krause, Ed Sharockman, Karl Kusselke and Earsell Mackbee. Grant, Tarkenton and Krause are in the Hall of Fame. Kassulke was left paralyzed in a 1973 motorcycle accident and died in 2008.

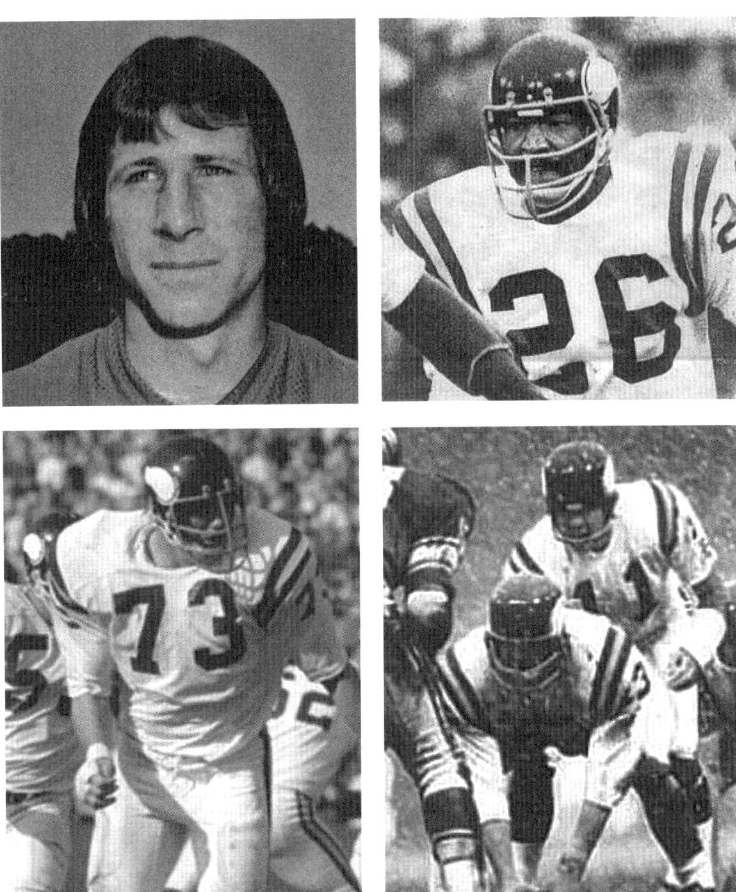

Clockwise from top left: Bob Grim, Clint Jones, Mick Tingelhoff (centering Joe Kapp) and Ron Yary. Grim was involved in both Tarkenton trades with the Giants.

Clockwise from top left: Chuck Foreman, John Gilliam, Sammy White and Ahmad Rashad helped form the first "West Coast" offense with Tarkenton and Bud Grant.

Clockwise from top left: Max Winter, Tarkenton on TV and The Purple People Eaters, Eller, Larson, Page and Marshall. Max Winter owned stakes in the Lakers and the Vikings..

The Vikings prepare for the 1975 Superbowl in New Orleans vs. Pittsburgh. The Vikings lost and there was a blizzard back home in what was to become the final years of the Tarkenton era of Vikings football.

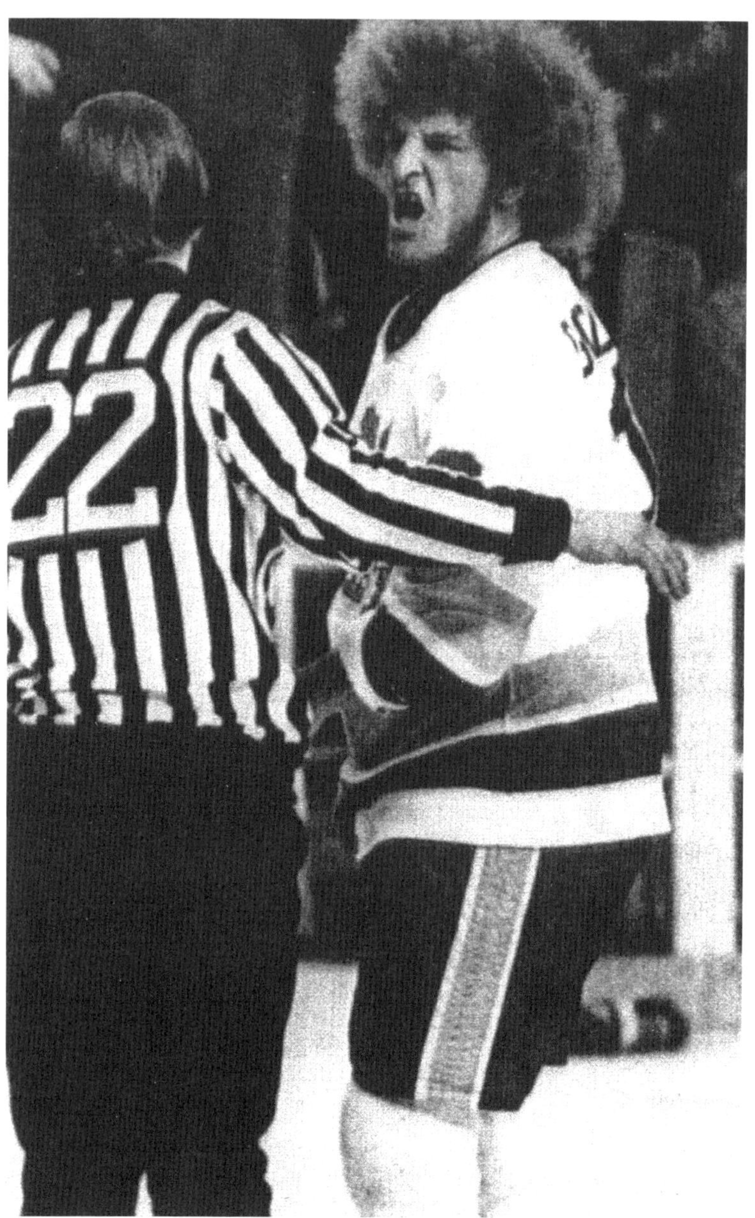

Fighting Saint Bill "Goldy" Goldthorpe.

Hockey's Bad Boys
The Minnesota Fighting Saints

Professional sports staked out its territory in the Twin Cities in the 1960s. In that decade the NFL's Vikings, MLB's Twins and the NHL's North Stars all set up shop in Bloomington, the Minneapolis suburb that found itself in the center of Minnesota's sports world. The only other competition for the sports dollar was in Minneapolis at the University of Minnesota. St. Paul felt a little left out.

Opportunity to join the ranks of pro sports came to St. Paul through the formation of a new hockey league, the World Hockey Association, organized by a sports entrepreneur named Dennis Murphy and his partner, tax attorney Gary Davidson, both from Orange County, California. With the financial backing and professional hockey contacts of Canadian Bill Hunter, Murphy and Davidson co-founded the WHA in 1971. With the help of Hunter, who had founded the Western Hockey League in Canada, the new league had solid prospects in Calgary, Winnipeg, Saskatoon and Edmonton.

Wayne Belisle, a local businessman, secured a WHA franchise for St. Paul while working with city officials to accommodate the team. The team was named the Minnesota Fighting Saints and was set to begin its inaugural season at the 8,500-seat St. Paul Auditorium in 1972.

The World Hockey Association plan was simple. They sought to establish WHA franchises in cities where no NHL teams existed and in cities large enough to accommodate two teams. To entice players onto their rosters, the World Hockey Association teams offered more money than the NHL in some cases, and did away with the NHL's reserve clause which bound players to teams after their contract had expired. For talent, the WHA relied on cast-offs from the NHL, college players and minor leaguers that hadn't quite made it. This usually equated to American players, a reality that the league used to spin a home-grown angle in their promotion.

The league's first big splash came with the signing of Bobby Hull from the Chicago Black Hawks, considered the greatest left winger to ever play the game. Responding to a comment Hull made regarding the WHA—that he might consider a jump to the new league for a million dollars—Winnipeg Jets owner Ben Hatskin offered just that for Hull to join his team. Hull gave the league instant credibility. In another coup for the WHA, Gordie Howe, who led the Detroit Red Wings to four Stanley Cups, was signed by the Houston Aeros. Wayne Gretzky would later sign his first pro contract with the WHA.

Sports fans in St. Paul, however, didn't need marquee names to appreciate good hockey. The Fighting Saints opted to put their team together around personnel who knew the game. To run the team, the Fighting Saints hired Glen Sonmor to manage and coach. As a player, Sonmor kicked around the minor leagues before ending up with the New York Rangers. He coached the Minnesota Gophers team before coming to the Fighting Saints, replaced at Minnesota by Herb Brooks. On the ice, the Saints signed NHL veterans such as Wayne Connelly, Ted Hampson, John Arbour, Mike McMahon, Mel Pearson and Terry Ball. Added to the mix were former college players and others with little or no pro experience, most notably Mike Antonovich who played for Sonmor at the "U" and went on to become the team's career leader in games played. In a move that was undoubtedly more of a promotional stunt than actual offer, the Saints drafted former Team USA Olympian Wendell Anderson, then Governor of Minnesota. Anderson declined the offer but the move helped to solidify the team's standing in the community. Saints players from Minnesota included Henry Boucha, Mike Curran and Keith Christiansen.

As their name would suggest, the Minnesota Fighting Saints liked to do just that. The team built its reputation around a tough and gritty brand of hockey. Front teeth were as rare as helmets on a team recognized as the most rugged in their league in an era when hockey was still a blood sport. In their first season of play, the Fighting Saints did well enough in the standings to finish fourth in their division and make it to the second round of playoffs. To fans of the team, the Saints' physical play was as important as wins or losses.

At the midpoint of the first season, the team moved from the St. Paul Auditorium to the state-of-the-art St. Paul Civic Center, which featured clear dasher boards. Though the club drew well at the relatively intimate auditorium, relying on the support of "true" hockey fans, the larger Civic Center would prove harder to fill. Regardless, the Fighting Saints continued to cultivate their tough reputation by adding more physical players to the roster.

By the second season Harry Neale was the full-time coach while Glen Sonmor moved to the front office full time. For the next season, the team added Gordie "Machine Gun" Gallant as their standout tough guy, a hatchet man who came to further exemplify the team's style of play. Gordie's charisma made him a fan favorite but his career with the Saints lasted just two years. The night before a playoff game, incensed by being checked on by Coach Neale at curfew, Gallant went to the coach's hotel room and fought with both Neale and assistant Jack McCarten. Gordie was dropped from the team the next morning. Still, Sonmor, who lost an eye to the butt end of a hockey stick during his playing days, loved tough players, and Gallant's intensity, tenacity and menacing appearance opened the doors for more of his kind.

The Saints were the brawlers of the WHA. In the course of their existence, they put together teams that included celebrated enforcers in the enigmatic Carlson brothers of Virginia, Minnesota, "Wild" Bill Goldthorpe, Curt Brackenbury, Bill Butters, Dave "Killer" Hanson, John McKenzie, Ron Busniuk, and Paul Holmgren. Goldthorpe was especially renowned in his career with the Fighting Saints, playing only three games, scoring no points and racking up twenty-five penalty minutes.

To fans, Jack, Steve and Jeff Carlson were too good to be true. With their thick black glasses and relentless style of play, they inspired the characters of the Hansen brothers in the movie *Slapshot* starring the late Paul Newman. While Steve and Jeff appeared in the film, Jack's role was filled by teammate Dave Hanson when Jack was called to play for the Edmonton Oilers. Along with the Bill Goldthorpe-inspired character Olgie Oldthorpe, the movie celebrated the Fighting Saints'—and WHA's—colorful brand of hockey. In one sequence of the film, teams began brawling during the warmup only to return to the ice bloodied and battered to sing the National Anthem to start the contest.

Jack Carlson played for the Saints for three years before moving to the NHL, and was the most famous of all WHA tough guys for his gritty play and hockey prowess. The Saints' line with Carlson, the talented Mike "Shakey" Walton and Paul Holmgren is regarded as one of the toughest of all time. Carlson's legend was furthered by a brawl in a 1975 playoff faceoff with the New England Whalers and their enforcer Nick Fotiu.

In the overtime match with the Whalers, the Saints came out flat in the first period. Sonmor called a meeting in the first intermission with Coach Neale, Bill Butters, Curt Brackenberry and Carlson, instructing them to "get something going." No sticks were needed on the opening drop of the second period. Instead, the gloves came off. Brackenberry started fighting immediately, opening the door for Butters to let loose on a Whalers player. With that, the benches cleared, creating an opportunity for Carlson and Fotiu, a former New York state boxing champion, to go at it. In a fight that lasted almost fifteen minutes the two beat each other unmercifully. Finally they decided to call it quits, and when Fotiu dropped his hands, Carlson ended the fight with a punch that sent the Whaler to the ice.

Through it all, the Fighting Saints made it to the playoffs in each of their first three years in the league. Though known for their physical play, they also enjoyed the scoring abilities of Connelly, Walton, and Antonovich. Despite their success, however, financial mismanagment led to the team's demise in the middle of the '75-76 season. But, as became common in the WHA, another league team, the recently-defunct Cleveland Crusaders, filled the void and were billed as the "New Fighting Saints."

The new team made news by signing Toronto Maple Leafs Hall of Fame star Dave Keon, while he was in the midst of some nasty negotiations with his former club. Despite his presence, the Saints II, who used red and gold uniforms in place of the familiar blue and gold, folded for good in January 1977.

Some former Fighting Saints went on to the NHL and international play. Mike Antonovich spent time with three NHL teams and three World Championship teams. Jack Carlson played for the North Stars and St. Louis Blues. His NHL highlight happened in 1981 as the North Stars advanced to the Stanley Cup finals. Jack played in only fifteen games, but is remembered for a night against Boston where he set a team record with 48 penalty minutes in one game.

WHA co-founder Gary Davidson also pursued expansion leagues in professional basketball with the ABA (remember the red, white and blue balls?) and in football with the World Football League. For a period in the '70s he managed all three leagues at the same time.

When the WHA folded in 1979, four of its strongest franchises joined the NHL. The Edmonton Oilers, New England Whalers (Carolina Hurricanes), Quebec Nordiques (Colorado Avalanche), and Winnipeg Jets (Phoenix Coyotes) all became expansion franchises. In St. Paul, after an absence of over twenty years, professional hockey lives again. After the North Stars moved to Dallas in 1993, the NHL granted a new franchise, the Minnesota Wild, to the city in 2000.

Clockwise from top left: The skilled George Morrison and the Carlson brothers—Jack, Jeff and Steve—added to the legend of the Fighting Saints.

MINNESOTA FIGHTING SAINTS — 1972-73

FRONT ROW (left to right): Don Niederkorn Equipment Manager; Carl Wetzel; George Konik; Ted Hampson, Captain; Glen Sonmor, General Manager/Coach; Mike Curran; Harry Neale, Assistant General Manager/Coach; Wayne Connelly, Alternate Captain; John Arbour, Alternate Captain; Jack McCartan; Glen Gostick, Trainer.

BACK ROW (left to right): Bill Rhody, Assistant Equipment Manager; Mike Antonovich; Bob MacMillan; Mel Pearson; Jim Johnson; Craig Falkman; Frank Sanders; Terry Ryan; Mike McMahon; Terry Ball; Blaine Rydman; Bill Klatt; Bill Young; Dick Paradise; George Morrison; Len Lilyholm; Keith Christiansen; Len Vannelli, Travelling Secretary.

Top: The talented and enigmatic Mike "Shakey" Walton.
Bottom: The original Fighting Saints from their first season, 1972-73

Clockwise from top left: Glen Sonmor, Harry Neale, Mike Curran and John Garrett. Neale and Sonmor, together with owner Wayne Belisle, managed the Saints. Curran and Garrett minded the nets.

Clockwise from top left: The movie *Slapshot* had Saints connections; Gordie "Machine Gun" Gallant (as a Quebec Nordique) and Curt Brackenbury put the fight in Fighting Saints; Mike Antonovich starred for the Saints.

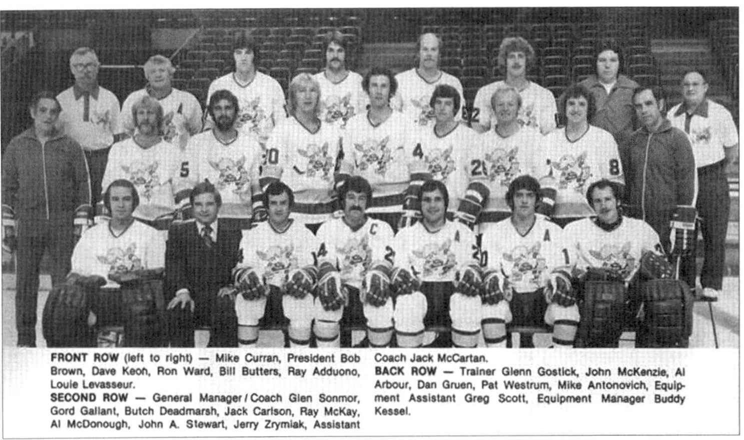

FRONT ROW (left to right) — Mike Curran, President Bob Brown, Dave Keon, Ron Ward, Bill Butters, Ray Adduono, Louie Levasseur.
SECOND ROW — General Manager / Coach Glen Sonmor, Gord Gallant, Butch Deadmarsh, Jack Carlson, Ray McKay, Al McDonough, John A. Stewart, Jerry Zrymiak, Assistant Coach Jack McCartan.
BACK ROW — Trainer Glenn Gostick, John McKenzie, Al Arbour, Dan Gruen, Pat Westrum, Mike Antonovich, Equipment Assistant Greg Scott, Equipment Manager Buddy Kessel.

Top: Dave Keon and Johnny "Pie" Mc Kenzie were NHL stars who played for the Saints in the team's last years. Bottom: The last Saints team, 1976-77.

From Worst to First
The Minnesota Twins' Improbable World Series Championship of 1991

"We'll see you tomorrow night."
–Commentator Jack Buck after Kirby Puckett's ninth-inning home run won Game Six in the 1991 World Series

The world was changing in the Spring of 1991. The United States had just entered into its first war with Iraq at the beginning of the year, and the Soviet Union collapsed. Kurt Cobain's band Nirvana introduced "grundge rock" to mainstream audiences and Michael Jordan won his first championship with the Chicago Bulls. Minnesota sports fans had the North Stars in the Stanley Cup and were looking forward to hosting the NCAA Final Four Men's Basketball Tournament at the Metrodome.

1991 was also the year that held a big surprise. It was the year of the "Cinderella Series," when two of the previous year's least successful Major League Baseball teams made it to the World Series.

For the Minnesota Twins and Atlanta Braves, the only thing that seemed to join the two as the baseball season began was their designations as last-place teams in their divisions the year before. Prospects for the upcoming year were dim.

The task ahead for the Twins was daunting: how to compete with a division rival Chicago White Sox powerhouse that included Jack McDowell, Frank Thomas, Carlton Fisk,

Robin Ventura and a young Sammy Sosa in their lineup. The Sox had won the division going away in 1990 as the Twins brought up the rear.

Three years after winning the World Series in 1987, stars Kirby Puckett and Kent Hrbek remained with the Twins but Gary Gaetti had left in the off-season. '87 hero Tom Brunansky was gone. Everyday players Dan Gladden, Greg Gagne, Brian Harper, and Scott Leius were still around but a lot of holes were left to fill.

To bolster their hitting, Manager Tom Kelly brought in designated hitter Chili Davis from the Angels and third baseman Mike Pagliarulo from the Padres. Both of those players had made their names with longer stints on other teams—the Giants and Yankees respectively—and were nearing the end of their careers. Fourth-year pro Shane Mack was also brought in from the Padres to play right field. Kelly went with a rookie, Chuck Knoblauch, to play second base. The biggest trade news came with the signing of St. Paul native Jack Morris after thirteen prominent years with the Detroit Tigers.

If the media and fans in the Twin Cities didn't expect much from the home team that year, the addition of the new players didn't change that view much. Opinions were especially mixed on the addition of the veteran Morris. Glad to have him in a Twins' uniform, many still wondered if he was past his prime.

If the Twins' outlook was not very optimistic, the Braves' fortunes seemed dismal. Fan favorite Dale Murphy, a perennial all-star playing for a bad franchise throughout his career, had retired after the 1990 season. The Braves had become used to losing, their 95 losses the previous year something of an accomplishment after losing 106 in 1988. The Braves were last in the league in attendance by a long shot in 1990, a fact that couldn't have made owner Ted Turner, also owner of the TBS television network, very happy. Things were so bad that one game at Atlanta-Fulton County Stadium drew less than 1,000 fans. A joke going around town at the time went something like this: *"Someone broke into my car in the parking garage last night—busted my window, stole my stereo and left me six Braves tickets."*

Additionally, Atlanta's off-season trades were even less remarkable than those of the Twins. With the acquisition of Otis Nixon from the Montreal Expos, Brian Hunter at first base, and outfielder Deion Sanders as part of a well-promoted experiment that also allowed him to play defensive back for the Atlanta Falcons football team, the Braves didn't figure to play far into the fall.

As the season began, the lackluster Twins seemed to confirm predictions. Luckily for the Twins, the Minnesota North Stars went on a roll. As the baseball club waddled through the first two months of the season, the local hockey franchise was steaming through the playoffs on its way to the Stanley Cup Finals. Finishing next to last in its division the year before and living with threats from team owner Norm Green to move the club, the North Stars captured the local imagination with a stirring playoff run.

By the time the North Stars had finished their season as Finals' runner up with a deflating 8-0 loss to the Pittsburgh Penguins, fans turned their attention to the early days of a Twins season of low expectations and shrugged. Yes, Chuck Knoblauch was raising some eyebrows with his crisp play at second and surprising hitting; Jack Morris still seemed to have some baseball left in him; and pitcher Scott Erickson, a respectable 8-4 the year before, was unhittable out of the gate. But the team's play was too inconsistent, and they struggled to a .500 record in April and May, staring up at Oakland, Seattle and Chicago in the standings.

Then came June.

In June of 1991 the Minnesota Twins compiled a record of 22-6 that gained them first-place standing in the American League West. The month began with a fifteen-game winning streak that, as it went along, attracted fans back to the club and drew national attention. By the break, the Twins had a comfortable lead in their division, and had three players on the All Star team: Kirby Puckett, Jack Morris and closer Rick Aguilera. Scott Erickson, turning in scintillating performances and winning twelve straight games through the first half of the year, was scheduled to be the starting pitcher for the American League, but was injured against Chicago at the end of June and couldn't play.

Through that period the Twins found their team identity. Kirby Puckett, batting champ the previous two seasons, was hitting over .300 and sparkled in center field in what would be a Gold Glove year. The infield with Pagliarulo and Scott Leius at third, Greg Gagne at short, Knoblauch (who would go on to earn Rookie of the Year honors) and Kent Hrbek at first base, gelled. In the outfield, surprising Shane Mack was also hitting over .300, while Dan Gladden was solid in left field. Chili Davis earned his pay, delivering the clutch hitting the Twins wanted from him. Catcher Brian Harper ran the defense behind the plate and was also hitting over .300. The pitching rotation of Jack Morris, Kevin

Tapani, and Scott Erickson was as good as any in the AL and Rick Aguilera was a solid closer, earning 42 saves. The Twins would win the division going away, by a comfortable eight-game margin. In doing so, they played against type, easily taking season series from the New York Yankees and Boston Red Sox while losing them against the White Sox and Toronto Blue Jays.

Meanwhile, in the National League, the Braves team made strides early with a 17-9 record in May—enough to boost their dismal attendance and give Ted Turner something to crow about—and promote. The team finished the halfway mark at .500—respectable given their recent past, and attendance began to grow. After the All Star break, the Braves went on a tear, winning their division by a game over a relentless L.A. Dodger squad. The Braves also found their identity in a starting pitching rotation of John Smoltz, Steve Avery and Tom Glavine, who dominated their league as few had done before. Veterans Lonnie Smith, Terry Pendleton and Otis Nixon pulled the team together with savvy play and leadership. Ron Gant, Jeff Treadway and David Justice had banner years, as Minnesota native Greg Olson anchored the Braves at catcher.

In the AL Championship the Twins easily dispatched the Toronto Blue Jays, the team that had owned them during the regular season. The Braves had a more difficult time defeating the Pittsburgh Pirates in seven games to win the National League crown.

The "Cinderella Series" was on.

Ted Turner, with his wife, actress Jane Fonda, added star power to the series as they rooted for their team from the stands and joined in the politically incorrect "Tomahawk

Chop" that rallied Braves fans and drew the ire of the rest of the country. The Twins fans, for their part, revived the "Homer Hankies" from the 1987 Series and hoped for a return of home-field advantage within the "Homer Dome." Minnesota was buzzing with excitement as a national audience grew to watch what was to be one of the greatest series of all time.

Twins manager Tom Kelly elected to go with a three-man pitching rotation for the Series, putting the workload and Game One starting responsibilities on Jack Morris. Morris pitched ten complete games in 1991 and Kelly was betting on his durability in the event of a seven-game series. Braves manager Bobby Cox inserted Charlie Liebrandt, an ex-Royals pitcher, into a rotation of his three pitching stars. The Series began at the Metrodome with Liebrandt getting the unexpected nod for the first game.

The Twins won the first two games at home, with Morris and Tapani holding serve. True to "Homer Dome" form, the Twins got home runs from Greg Gagne, Kent Hrbek, Chili Davis and Scott Leius against none for the Braves, as the Twins sent the Series back to Atlanta with a 2-0 lead. Hrbek set the tone for the series in Game Two, as Atlanta's Ron Gant was picked off at first. Hrbek, in a move that would make a pro wrestler proud, took the throw from pitcher Kevin Tapani and lifted Gant off first base to apply the tag.

Game Three in Atlanta was an extra-inning affair that saw Rick Aguilera give up the game winner in the 12th inning. The next game was another one-run victory for the Braves that tied the teams at two games apiece. Throughout those games the Twins went deep into their bullpen to no avail. When Game Five in Atlanta rolled around, the bullpen had nothing left and the Braves won in a laugher, 14-5, sending things back to Minneapolis with a 3-2 lead over a shell-shocked Minnesota club.

The play of Kirby Puckett in Game Six of the 1991 World Series is not the only reason he is still regarded as one of the most popular sports figures in Minnesota history but it did add to his lore. The team was reeling after losing three straight in Atlanta. Game Six had Kevin Tapani starting against Steve Avery at the Dome—a tossup—and the Twins were looking for answers against Atlanta's pitchers. The games had now become grudge matches and the intensity was palpable.

Puckett started things off by tripling home Chuck Knoblauch in the first inning and scoring when Shane Mack singled to give the Twins the early lead. In the third inning, Kirby robbed Ron Gant of a home run with a highlight-reel backhanded catch above the fence. When Terry Pendleton hit a two-run blast in the fifth to tie the game, Puckett answered with a sacrifice fly to retake the lead. The Braves scored a run in the seventh inning to tie the score again.

As the game went on, neither team could score and the tension in the stadium continued to grow. Charlie Liebrandt was on the mound for Atlanta when Puckett led off for the Twins in the bottom of the eleventh. Since Liebrandt was a former Kansas City Royal, the two had faced each other many times, with Kirby having much success. The Metrodome erupted when Puckett sent a 2-1 pitch into the center field stands to send the Series to a seventh game.

But Kirby Puckett was not the MVP of the 1991 World Series. That honor went to Jack Morris after his heroics in the seventh game. Game Seven featured Morris against John Smoltz on the mound for the Braves. The pitchers cruised through the early innings with no score. Morris pitched out of a jam in the fifth to keep the game scoreless. The Braves blew a chance in the eighth when Lonnie Smith committed a base running error and again Morris pitched out of the inning. After nine innings of the seventh game of the Series, neither team had scored and Morris was still on the mound.

For the tenth, Tom Kelly looked to Rick Aguilera to take over the game but Morris strongly objected. Kelly relented and Morris took the field. With overpowering will and determination, he retired the Braves in just eight pitches and handed the game to the offense. After Dan Gladden, Puckett and Hrbek loaded the bases in the bottom of the inning, Gene Larkin hit a long fly to score Gladden and the game was over. Jack Morris had just pitched a ten-inning shutout to win the World Series.

The parade in Minneapolis after the win was an outpouring of celebration and adoration for the Twins as thousands of fans turned out. A gloomy year had turned to gold, and the Minnesota Twins were the unlikely champions of Major League Baseball. In the following weeks Minnesota was struck by the Halloween blizzard as Jack Morris departed for the Toronto Blue Jays. But the memory of one of the greatest seasons and World Series of all time lives on in the Gopher State.

Kent Hrbek and Jack Morris celebrate after Game Seven.

1991 Minnesota Twins World Series Roster

Rick Aguilera
Steve Bedrosian
Jarvis Brown
Randy Bush
Chili Davis
Scott Erickson
Greg Gagne
Dan Gladden
Mark Guthrie
Brian Harper
Kent Hrbek
Chuck Knoblauch
Gene Larkin
Terry Leach
Scott Leius
Shane Mack
Jack Morris
Al Newman
Junior Ortiz
Mike Pagliarulo
Kirby Puckett
Paul Sorrento
Kevin Tapani
David West
Carl Willis

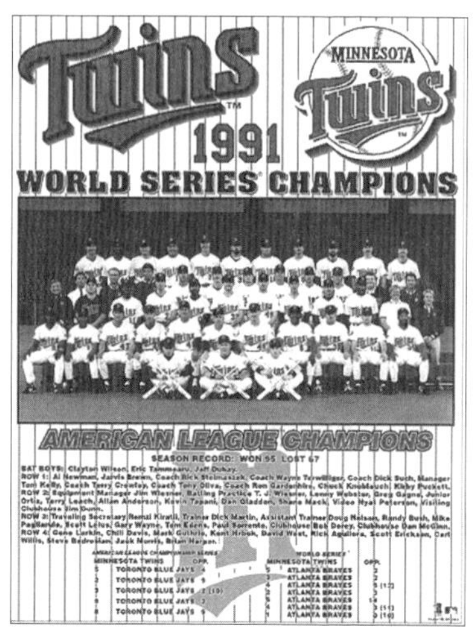

The Twins played .500 ball through May then streaked to first in June at the Metrodome.

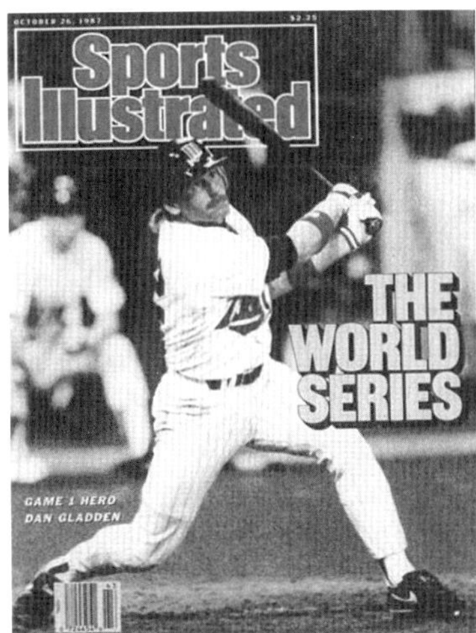

Clockwise from top left: Dan Gladden on the cover of *Sports Illustrated*, Mike Pagliarulo, Gene Larkin and Chili Davis.Pagliarulo and Davis shipped in from New York and LA rsepectively to contribute to the title.

Clockwise from top left: Scott Erickson, Kent Hrbek, Chuck Knoblauch and Shane Mack each played critical roles during the season and the playoffs.

1991 Atlanta Braves World Series Roster

Steve Avery	Kent Mercker
Rafael Belliard	Keith Mitchell
Jeff Blauser	Greg Olson
Sid Bream	Alejandro Pena
Francisco Cabrera	Terry Pendleton
Jim Clancy	Lonnie Smith
Ron Gant	John Smoltz
Tom Glavine	Mike Stanton
Tommy Gregg	Randy St. Claire
Brian Hunter	Jeff Treadway
David Justice	Jerry Willard
Charlie Leibrandt	Mark Wohlers
Mark Lemke	

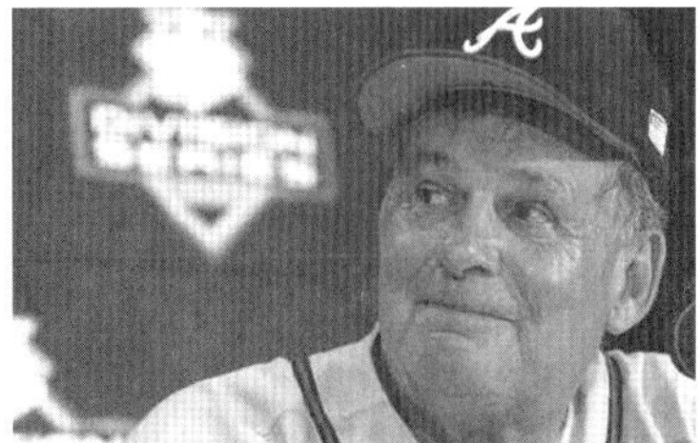

Bobby Cox lead the Braves to the Series at Atlanta's now-demolished Fulton County Stadium where owner Ted Turner and Jane Fonda led fans in the Tomahawk Chop.

Excitement filled the dome and all of Minnesota as the Series began.

Game 6: Charlie Liebrandt, Kirby Puckett and "We'll see you tomorrow night."

Top: Jack Morris pitched a complete Game Seven over manager Tom Kelly's objection.
Bottom: The Twins celebrate the victory.

Top: Tom Kelly and owner Carl Pohlad accept the trophy as the Twins were crowned champions.
Bottom: Pandemonium reigned during the downtown Minneapolis victory parade.

Jack Morris

The seeds of Jack Morris' baseball career were sown on the dusty fields of St. Paul's playgrounds. St. Paul of the 1960s had an active park in every parish where kids would spend summer days playing pickup games, while playing each other in organized leagues at night. Morris played at Edgcumbe playground, a baseball hotbed near parks that boasted future major leaguers Dave Winfield and Paul Molitor. Jack Morris was a hard-throwing third baseman/ pitcher who played along side his younger brother Tom, a left-handed curveball pitcher and playground legend as they entered Highland Park High School. The Morris brothers helped Highland to titles in both basketball and baseball as both caught baseball scouts' attention. Jack Morris was a raw talent who threw uncontolled heat as he and his brother graduated to Utah's Brigham Young University, where Jack would develop a split finger fastball and control. While brother Tom's baseball career would end in the minors, Jack Morris combined expert pitching and an in-your-face attitude to thrive in the majors, first for Detroit then hitting his zenith in Game Seven of the 1991 World Series, pitching his hometown Twins to victory over the Atlanta Braves. Morris' baseball career ended as a St. Paul Saint in 1996.

Currently Morris keeps a home in Minnesota and provides commentary for Minnesota Twins broadcasts.

Jack Morris at Highland Park High School and Edgcumbe Playground, St. Paul's baseball hotbed in the 1960s and '70s.

Top: Jack Morris starred in basketball for Highland Park as did his brother Tom, pictured here (center) on the 1975 Highland baseball team. Bottom: Highland Park High School in the '70s. Both brothers went on to attend Brigham Young University where Tom Morris now teaches.

Clockwise from top left: Morris pitched for much of his career with the Detroit Tigers. After pitching the Twins to the title in 91 he did likewise for Toronto in 1992, later moving to Cleveland and finally back home with the St. Paul Saints in 1996.

Bill Goldsworthy

In the 1960s Minnesota was a new home to the NFL, American League baseball and, in 1967, NHL expansion. Added to the league's "Original 6" were six new teams including the Minnesota North Stars—and their "star" was Bill Goldsworthy. Goldsworthy was one of the players who climbed from the minors (drafted from the Boston Bruins system) to excel in the NHL's expansion era. A two-way team player, he possessed great vision and hands. These, with a winning smile and his "Goldy Shuffle" celebration combined to make Bill the face of the North Stars into the 1970s. Goldsworthy's career peaked in 1973-'74 with a 48 goal /74 point season. He went on to play for The New York Rangers and in the WHA, retiring in 1979. Bill later coached in amateur and minor league hockey. The North Stars retired his #8 in 1992 prior to moving to Dallas. Goldsworthy struggled with alcoholism during his life, and tragedy struck in 1994 when he was diagnosed with AIDS. He passed away in 1996.

Patty Berg

Everyone loved Patty Berg. The fresh-faced and plucky golfer from Minneapolis turned an amateur career of twenty-nine wins into a record-setting pro career and in the process was a founding member of the Ladies Professional Golf Association (LPGA) Tour. Her fifteen major-title wins remains the all-time record for the most by a female golfer.

She took up golf in 1931 and began her amateur career in 1934, winning the Minneapolis City Championship. She gained national attention when she reached the final of the 1935 U.S. Women's Amateur.

After winning twenty-nine amateur titles, she turned professional in 1940. During World War II she served in the Marines. In 1948, she became the first president of the LPGA. In her career, Berg won 57 events on the pro circuit. She was voted the Associated Press Woman Athlete of the Year in 1938, 1942 and 1955. Her last victory came in 1962.

She announced in December 2004 that she had been diagnosed with Alzheimer's disease and died in Fort Myers in 2006 at the age of 88.

Minnesota Kicks

In 1976, the baby boom was peaking, the drinking age was 18 and The Minnesota Kicks of the North American Soccer League arrived from Denver. These facts combined to create a brief but spectacular era of tailgating and partying at Metropolitan Stadium in the late '70s. Playing to capacity crowds, the likes of Alan Willey, Ace Ntsoelengue, Allen Merrick, Ron Futcher and Tino Lettieri entertained eager fans with soccer and spectacle, winning multi-division championships while in Minnesota. The Kicks folded in 1981 under financial pressure. The Minnesota Strikers played at the Metrodome and at the Met Center from 1984 -1988 with some former Kicks but failed to capture the magic of the 1970s.

The Minnesota Kicks played to capacity crowds at Met Stadium in the 1970s.

Clockwise from top: Alan Willey, Tino Letteri and Ace Ntsoelengue led the Kicks and Strikers during soccer's rise in Minnesota.

Dan Patch

Dan Patch was a superstar. The racehorse, living in Savage, Minnesota during his years of fame, lost only two heats in his whole career, and never lost a race. His achievements on the track also made him a sports figure of nearly unprecedented celebrity status, with front-page newspaper attention, numerous product endorsements, and books written about the big brown stallion. At his best, he earned over one million dollars a year. His influence was so great that in 1949 he even became the subject of a popular Hollywood film, *The Great Dan Patch*, decades after his death.

Foaled in 1896, Dan Patch broke world speed records at least fourteen times in his career. He set the official record for the pacing mile in Lexington, Kentucky in 1905 and seemingly bettered it by one quarter of a second a year later at the Minnesota State Fair in an unofficial record time of one minute, fifty-five seconds, a record that stood for 32 years. His speed was so great that other horse owners would sometimes refuse to race their horses against him, leaving Dan Patch to run against the clock.

The age of the automobile had not yet arrived so harness racing enjoyed huge popularity in the early 1900s. When Dan Patch traveled, courtesy of his custom-designed and luxurious rail car, crowds of up to 100,000 turned out to see him perform.

Dan Patch retired undefeated in 1909 to his home in Savage. He performed in exhibitions until his death in 1916.

Top: Dan Patch in his prime.
Bottom: The champion's home in Savage, Minn.

1991-92: In the Spotlight

In 1991 and '92 Minnesota hosted some of the top events in sports.

1991: The Stanley Cup: Pittsburgh beat the North Stars in six games; the U.S. Open was won by the late Payne Stewart at Hazeltine in Chaska and the Twins won the World Series in seven games.

1992: The Super Bowl: Washington beat Buffalo as St. Paul celebrated the Winter Carnival and Duke defeated Michigan for the title in the NCAA Final 4 at the Metrodome.

Minnesota's Good Sports

Left to right: Minnesota native Lee Meade was instrumental in the launch of the ABA and WHA, acting as PR Director and in various management positions for each league; Dick Jonckowski, "The Polish Eagle," is an announcer for numerous sports including baseball for the Minnesota Gophers; Ross Benstein, former Gopher hockey mascot, has written over 50 books on Minnesota sports.

Minnesota Sports on Screen

Clockwise from top left: *Ice Castles*, starring Robby Benson and Lynn Holly Johnson, was filmed in part in Waverly, Minn.; *Little Big League*, a '90s yarn about the Twins was shot in Edina; the three *Mighty Ducks* movies, shot at Minnesota rinks, spawned youth hockey interest nation wide; TV's *Coach* took place at the mythical Minnesota State University.

Stadiums and Arenas

Clockwise from top left: Lexington Park at University and Lexington in St. Paul; the Lexington Park site today; Nicollet Park, formerly near Lake and Nicollet in Minneapolis.

Top: "Old" Midway Stadium, just east of Snelling near Como in St. Paul, was built to house a major league team. The St. Paul Saints played there until disbanding to make way for the Twins. The park was torn down in the '80s. Bottom: The new Midway Stadium (just west of the old stadium) houses the revived Saints.

Clockwise from top: Metropolitan Stadium, torn down after the 1981 season, was home to the Millers, Twins, Vikings,and Kicks; the Mall of America replaced it. Wade Stadium, a classic in West Duluth was home to the Dukes and, currently, the Huskies baseball teams.

Top: The St. Paul Civic Center and Auditorium were home to high schools, minor league and major league teams including The Minnesota Fighting Saints and Minnesota Moose. The Civic Center was replaced by the Xcel Center, home of the Wild. Bottom: The Duluth Curling Club on London Road hosted high school games and was the first home of the Division 1 UMD Bulldogs hockey team. The building was replaced by the DECC near Canal Park.

Top: Memorial Stadium, home of the Gophers was torn down in 1981.
Bottom: No this is not a stadium or arena. This is one of several Quarterback Club Restaurants located throughout the Twin Cities and Minnesota in the '60s and '70s. The Northfield Club still exists sans football on the roof. The clubs were owned by a partnership of Minnesota athletes. (Courtesy Quarterback Club)

About the Author

Phil Tippin

Phil Tippin is layout designer of The Minnesota Series. He is a graduate of Louisiana State University where he developed a keen appreciation for sports while working at the training table for the LSU football and basketball teams. He also worked as art director for *City Pages* news weekly where he developed a keen appreciation for journalism and learned some of the vagaries of the publishing business. He has worked as a busboy, landscape installer, retail display designer, bass player, spotlight operator, roadie, set designer, house painter, florist, graphic designer, ad designer, event coordinator and chauffeur. While preparing content ideas for this book he convinced Minnesota Series' publishers to let him try his hand at writing *Sports Legends*. Phil now adds "author" to his list of accomplishments.

In Memorium

Dedicicated to the memory of Minnesota Vikings Wally Hilgenberg and Karl Kassulke.

Wally Hilgenberg

Karl Kassulke

Photo and Content Credits:

Cover and Chapters 1-8: Photo and content contributions courtesy of and special thanks to: The Chicago Historical Society, the Minnesota Vikings/NFL, the St. Paul Saints, Dick Jonckowski, U of M, Lee Meade, Minnesota Twins/ MLB, Duluth Huskies, Mike Krieter Photography: *Minnesota Ice Arenas*, Dale Finger, Quarterback Club Collection, D Media Services.

Coming Up Next in The Minnesota Series:

Don't miss our next book, *Celebrity Minnesota*, which chronicles the personalities that made our state famous. Read about **Jessica Lange**, **Judy Garland**, **Peter Graves**, **F. Scott Fitzgerald**, **Tippi Hedren**, **John Madden**, **Tiny Tim, the Coen Brothers, Josh Hartnett, Winona Ryder** and more in this edition of The Minnesota Series.

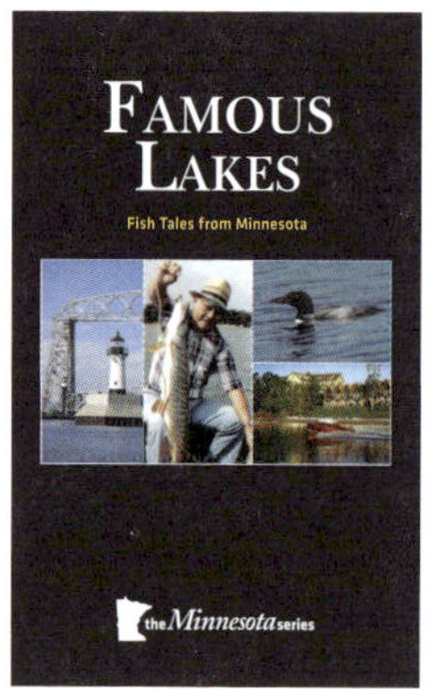

In *Famous Lakes*, read all about the folklore, fish tales and history of Minnesota's lakes and resort country. From Lake Wobegon to Lake of the Woods, Famous Lakes is a must-read for every Minnesotan who has fished, swam or just taken the pontoon for a cocktail cruise.

In *Political Stars*, read about famous families (the Mondales, Humphreys and Colemans), the "Rudys" (Perpich and Boschwitz), Minnesota's first congresswoman (Coya Knutson) and our most colorful governor ever (Jesse Ventura)–Minnesota politicians make for the most remarkable stories. **Don't miss these engaging tales as well as the inside stories of Eugene McCarthy, Paul Wellstone, Al Franken and others!**

Festivals & Events
Outdoors & Adventure
Lodging
Arts & Culture